GERALD R. FORD
1913-

Chronology - Documents - Bibliographical Aids

Edited by
GEORGE J. LANKEVICH

Series Editor
HOWARD F. BREMER

Oceana Publications, Inc.
Dobbs Ferry, New York
1977

For my parents George and Madeline Lankevich

Library of Congress Cataloging in Publication Data

Lankevich, George J.

   Gerald R. Ford, 1913-

   (Oceana presidential chronology series)
   Bibliography: p.
   Includes index.
   1. United States—Politics and government—1974-1977—Sources.
2. United States—Politics and government—1974-1977—Chronology.
3. Ford, Gerald R., 1913- I. United States. President, 1974-1977 (Ford).
E865.F67   973.925   77-8429

Manufactured in the United States of America

CONTENTS

EDITOR'S FOREWORD

Before 1976, Gerald Ford never aspired to be president of the United States. Although he won all but one election during his public life, all he ever wished to achieve was leadership of the House of Representatives. To be Speaker of "the people's House" was his fondest hope, for in the House he spent his happiest years. In the last three years of his public life, because of an unprecedented series of moral and political disasters, Ford attained two of his three public offices by appointment. He became vice president and then president of an America whose confidence and whose faith was shattered by political scandal and a lost war. Ford offered to his nation decency, candor and stability after the "nightmares" of Watergate and Vietnam. Over the course of thirty months he led our troubled nation and restored America's faith in the presidency and in our destiny. History may decree that his administration will merit only a cursory footnote, for Ford's legislative accomplishments were few. Stalemated government in Washington was obvious; we were expelled from the mainland of Asia; inflation, energy and employment problems went unresolved. Senator Hubert Humphrey savaged Ford's conservatism, calling him a "seventeenth century physician bleeding patients in an attempt to cure them" while Ralph Nader labeled him a "smiling man who makes cruel decisions" at the expense of America's poor. The president's vetoes often seemed to place him out of touch with the mainstream of American life. And finally, he became only the eighth incumbent president to lose an election.

Yet despite the unresolved debate on national purposes and governmental limits, Ford did play a critical role in American history: he restored to the nation a sense of its worth. Fate made him president, but his honor and character let him perform well a job which many thought would crush him. Americans who lived through the difficult years after 1974 may ponder Ford's policies but they share a conviction that almost surely will not fade with historical analysis: America was fortunate that Gerald Ford served as thirty-eighth president of the United States.

George J. Lankevich

EARLY LIFE AND CONGRESSIONAL APPRENTICESHIP

1913-1929   Leslie Lynch King is born in Omaha on July 14, 1913. After
             his parents divorce in 1915, his mother remarries and the
             boy is formally adopted by her new husband. Gerald R.
             Ford, Jr. grows up and is educated in the public schools
             of Michigan's second city, Grand Rapids, where his father
             operates the Ford Paint and Varnish Co.

1930-1931   Ford is twice an All-Star football player at South High School
             and is named "most popular senior" at graduation. He en-
             ters Michigan University in September, 1931.

1932-1934   After two years as substitute center on the undefeated Mi-
             chigan football teams of 1932-33, Ford becomes the Most
             Valuable Player on the poor team of 1934. In addition to his
             three varsity letters he is a member of Michigamua, an es-
             teemed senior honor.

1935   January. Ford plays in the East-West Shrine Game.

             June. The future President graduates from Michigan with
             a B.A. degree and a B average.

             August. After participating in the College All-Star Game,
             Ford declines two pro-football contracts.

             September. Ford begins six years as assistant coach in
             boxing and football at Yale University.

1938   September. Ford begins law study on a trial basis. He ul-
             timately graduates from Yale in the top third of his class.

1940   March. Look magazine runs an article on the "beautiful
             people" of Stowe, Vt. One of the models is Jerry Ford.

             Fall. Ford works as a volunteer in the Wilkie presidential
             campaign.

1941   After receiving his law degree from Yale and winning ad-
             mission to the Michigan Bar, Ford opens a law practice with
             Philip Buchan. He joins a reform Republican movement aim-
             ed at ousting local boss Frank McKay.

1942-1945   Ensign Ford joins the Navy. He serves forty-seven months
                 of active duty on carriers, primarily as a physical instruc-
                 tor, and is discharged as a Lieutenant Commander with ten
                 battle stars.

1946-1947   Ford works in the Grand Rapids law firm of Julius Amberg.
                 He is active in community affairs and organizes the Indepen-
                 dent Veterans Association to seek better housing facilities
                 for returned servicemen. He receives the Jay Cee Distin-
                 guished Service Award for that accomplishment (1948).

1948   June 17. Gerald Ford announces his candidacy for the House
                 seat held by Bartel Jonkman, a 64 year old Republican identi-
                 fied with McKay's machine. He campaigns on a platform of
                 aid to Europe and his youth as opposed to Jonkman's age.

                 September 14. Ford wins the Fifth Congressional District's
                 Republican primary with 23,632 votes to only 14,341 for the
                 four-term incumbent.

                 October 15. At the Grace Episcopal Church, Ford marries
                 Elizabeth Bloomer, a divorcee who once danced with the Mar-
                 tha Graham troupe.

                 November 2. Ford receives 60.5 per cent of the vote and wins
                 election to the Eighty-first Congress. He is perceived as a
                 young protege of Arthur Vandenberg. A hard working conserv-
                 ative, Ford will never lose an election in Michigan.

1949   January 3. As he is sworn into the House of Representatives,
                 Ford ranks 368th in seniority and is assigned to serve on the
                 Public Works Committee. His first vote is cast to liberalize
                 House rules by restricting "pigeon-holing" of legislation. By
                 the end of his first year he has voted against both minimum
                 wage and public housing laws, helped organize the Chowder
                 and Marching Club for House Republicans and been named one
                 of "America's Ten Outstanding Young Men."

1950   March 15. Michael Gerald Ford is born.

                 Ford adheres to the Republican position in 81 per cent of
                 his votes. His major achievement is an investigation of
                 the U.S. Army Corps of Engineers. His staff, led by John
                 P. Milanowski, efficiently deals with his district's needs.

                 November 7. Ford wins re-election with 66 per cent of
                 the vote in the 5th C.D.

1951   January. Ford joins the Appropriations Committee. He
becomes something of an expert on defense-budget spending and enhances his understanding of government operations. His second term proves him a "team player" as he
votes Republican 72 per cent of the time.

1952   February 22. Ford joins eighteen other Republican representatives in urging General Dwight D. Eisenhower to return to the United States and become a candidate for the
presidency.

       March 16. John Ford is born.

       November 4. Ford, having rejected an attempt at the Sen-
ate, is re-elected to the House with 66 per cent of the vote.
He has consistently advocated more military spending, less
foreign aid (except for Point Four) and has voted to deregulate natural gas prices.

1953-1954 Ford slowly advances up the seniority ladder and enhances
his position. He was an Eisenhower man before the Convention, is close friends with Vice President Richard Nixon
effectively serves on the Defense Appropriations Subcommittee, and declines to challenge for the seat of Republican
Senator Homer Ferguson. In November, 1954, he is again
re-elected with 63 per cent of his district's vote.

1955-1956 The Fords, seemingly committed to a Washington career,
build a home in Alexandria and welcome their third son,
Steven Meigs (May 19, 1956). Ford begins ten years of service on the CIA Appropriations Subcommittee, helps defeat
a "dump Nixon" movement within the party, declines the
opportunity to run for governor against Democrat G. Mennen
"Soapy" Williams, and wins an A. D. A. rating of 58.5 per
cent for the session. On November 6, 1956 he wins re-
election to the House with 67 per cent of the vote. The Democrats control Congress despite the Eisenhower landslide.

1957-1958 The greatest achievement of Ford's fifth House term is the
birth of his daughter, Susan Elizabeth, on July 6, 1957. The
election of November 4, 1958 reduces Republican strength
in the House by forty-six seats, but Ford personally wins a
sixth term by easily defeating Richard C. VanderVeen.

1959-1960 As the Eighty-sixth Congress convenes, Ford joins the insur-
rection that removes Joseph Martin as Republican leader and

replaces him with Charles Halleck. He is named by Sports
Illustrated as one of twenty-five football players who "con-
tributed the most to their fellow citizens; but he has not
been responsible for any major legislation. In July, 1960,
Ford seconds the nomination of Henry Cabot Lodge for Vice
President. The Republican ticket loses to John Kennedy, but
Ford (now seventeenth in seniority) is re-elected with 67
per cent of his district's vote.

1961-1962   Ford, now the ranking Republican on the Defense Appropriations Subcommittee and second on Foreign Operations, supports Kennedy's foreign aid initiatives. The American Political Science Association designates him a "congressman's
congressman." In the elections of November 6, 1962, Republican strength is further reduced, but Ford wins 67
per cent of his district's vote.

1963   January 2. A Republican caucus revolution led by Charles
Goodell and Robert Griffin succeeds in naming Ford Conference Chairman, ousting sixty-seven year old Charles
Hoeven. The vote is 86-78 as Jerry Ford, as always,
proves "electable."

November 22. John Fitzgerald Kennedy is assassinated in
Dallas.

November 29. Lyndon Johnson, in Executive Order 11130,
names Gerald Ford to the seven-member Warren Commission which investigates the death of JFK.

December 5. The Warren Commission holds the first of
thirteen Executive Sessions. The issue of FBI or CIA ties
to the assassin dominates its discussions. On December
16, Ford attacks the FBI's summary; it "did not have the
depth that it ought to have."

1964   June 4. At an Executive Session of the Warren Commission,
Ford questions the assumption that one man alone assassinated JFK. "I have some personal conclusions, but I cannot prove them, so I don't want to make any allegations."

June 29. Ford addresses the House on "American Strategy and
and Strength." His speech stridently denounces accommodation with Russia and attacks Johnson's "why win" policy.

July 15. Ford nominates Michigan Governor George Romney
for president. Perhaps this costs Ford the vice presidency,

for Barry Goldwater obtains a first ballot nomination.

September 27. The Warren Commission publishes its conclusion that one man alone assassinated JFK.

October 28. Ford travels to Warsaw, Indiana to praise Minority Leader Charles Halleck.

November 3. In the face of LBJ's electoral landslide, Ford
wins 61 per cent of his district's vote.

December 19. After meeting with insurgents, led by Goodell
and Griffin, Ford announces his candidacy for minority leader. He promises to achieve "better communication of the
Republican message through new techniques and bold leadership."

1965   January 4. Ford is elected minority leader, by a vote of
73-67, and promises to work for "positive Republican alternative programs." In concert with Senator Everett Dirksen,
Ford holds a series of anti-LBJ press conferences, the "Ev
and Jerry Show."

March. Ford fails in seventeen attempts to amend the Ap-
palachian Development Bill.

June. The minority leader's appearances supporting Republican candidates have already taken him to thirty-two states,
but he refuses to appear in Natchez before an all-white audience. Ford receives honorary doctorates from three col-
leges, and becomes an author with Portrait of the Assassin.

July. Congress rejects four of Ford's "positive" alternatives,
including a weakened Civil Rights Bill. Grand Rapids' newspapers accuse Ford of voting only for the final version of
bills (fair housing, Civil Rights) which he worked to kill
before passage. Johnson accuses Ford of playing football
for too long "without a helmet."

Ford begins to display his competence as minority leader;
from 1965 - 74 he was always able to deliver 85 per cent to
95 per cent of the Republican vote.

1966   April. Ford attacks "Johnson inflation" and mismanagement
of the Vietnam war. He also demands a congressional investigation of UFO's, a request mercifully buried.

May. Ford receives the George Washington Award from
the Good Government Society.

October. Johnson's trip to Asia is denounced by Ford as
a "political gimmick."

November 8. Ford wins his easiest re-election, obtaining 68 per cent of the Fifth District's vote.

1967   January. Ford delivers a "Republican State of the Union"
speech and proposes forty-four "sensible solutions for the
seventies." He soon casts votes against OEO, Model Cities,
and rent control.

February 10. The Twenty-Fifth Amendment to the Constitution is adopted.

August. In his speeches Ford asks, "Why are we pulling
our best punches in Vietnam?" He always remains a hawk
on the war in Southeast Asia.

1968   March 6. Ford praises Nixon's Vietnam position, saying
his "record speaks for itself in support of our national objectives." After the Tet offensive, however, Ford advocates
Americanization of the war effort.

April 11. Goodell convinces Ford to "reassess" his opposition to open housing legislation and he votes for its final
passage.

June. Ford receives three more honorary degrees.

August. At the Republican Convention in Miami Beach, Ford
serves as Permanent Chairman and uses the podium to attack
LBJ's war and America's military decline. Richard Nixon
is nominated for the presidency and Spiro T. Agnew completes the ticket.

September 10-12. Ford condemns Agnew's charge that Democratic nominee Hubert Humphrey is "soft" on Communism
and forces an Agnew apology.

November 5. Nixon is elected president but Republicans
win only four additional House seats. Ford, though re-
elected, recognizes he will never be Speaker.

December 4. Ford laments the urban crisis saying, "The question - Who does what and how? And how will the action program be paid for?"

1969   January 20. Melvin Laird becomes secretary of defense, and his former aide, Robert Hartmann joins Ford's staff.

April. Ford endorses G. Gordon Liddy for a job with the Department of Transportation. His congressional stance remains one of opposition as he casts votes to reduce federal aid to education and to limit the Voting Rights Act.

September 3. Nixon nominates Clement Haynsworth to the Supreme Court.

November 7. Ford announces his investigation of Justice William Douglas' fitness to serve on the Court.

November 21. Haynsworth is rejected by the Senate, 55-45.

December 12. The attorney general's office provides Ford with FBI information harmful to Justice Douglas.

1970   April 15. Ford calls for the impeachment of Douglas; "an impeachable offense is whatever a majority of the House of Representatives considers it to be at a given moment in history." His demand is made only a week after the Senate rejected Nixon's second nominee to the Court.

June 22. Ford calls the invasion of Cambodia a "tremendous military success."

Fall. Defying the White House, Ford supports Charles Goodell's race for the Senate seat from New York.

November 3. Goodell loses to Conservative candidate James Buckley. Ford is re-elected after a bitter campaign.

November 16. Ford declares that Nixon respected Cambodia's neutrality although he was fully aware of our two year bombing campaign against that nation. Ford states that there is "nothing false or deceptive in the information that has come from the White House."

In 1970, Ford reports his all-time high in lecture fees, $47,000.

1971   Honors are awarded to Ford by the American Veterans and
            the Academy of Achievement; the Conservative Coalition
            calls his voting record eighty-seven per cent right. However,
            Nixon's domestic advisor, John Ehrlichman, reportedly calls
            Ford a "jerk" and a "Nixon yo-yo." As minority leader, Ford
            supports the imposition of a wage/price freeze and denounces
            public outrage at increased fighting in Vietnam.

1972   May 2. J. Edgar Hoover, director of the FBI, dies. Reve-
            lations about agency abuses of power will plague Ford's
            presidency.

            June 17. The Watergate Headquarters of the Democratic
            party is burglarized.

            June 23-July 7. Ford tours the People's Republic of China.
            He describes the Chinese people as "clean, healthy, strong,
            industrious, disciplined and highly motivated."

            August 19-22. Ford presides over Republican Convention
            that re-nominates the Nixon/Agnew ticket.

            September 15. Nixon decides that Minority Leader Ford
            must be urged to limit the House's investigation of Water-
            gate and comments that Jerry has "got to get at this and
            screw this thing up."

            October 3. Wright Patman's committee votes 20-14 against
            asking subpoena powers to advance its Watergate inquiries.

            November 7. Despite the Nixon landslide, the Republican
            party does not come near a House majority. Ford, over-
            whelmingly elected despite nursing a knee operation, is
            now certain he will never be Speaker and contemplates
            retirement.

                          THE VICE PRESIDENCY

1973   February 7. The Senate, by a vote of 70-0, names a com-
            mittee to investigate the Watergate affair.

            April 16. Ford urges all administration officials to "go
            before the Senate Committee, take an oath and deny [com-
            plicity] publicly."

April 30. Ford terms the forced resignations of Robert Haldeman, John Ehrlichman and John Dean "a necessary first step in clearing the air." His faith in Nixon is unwavering and the Congressional Quarterly finds that he supports the president on 83 per cent of policy votes.

May 25. Archibald Cox is appointed Special Watergate Prosecutor.

August 2-8. Vice President Agnew, officially informed of a Baltimore Grand Jury inquiry into his finances, meets with the president, tells the press of the inquiry and asserts he will not resign.

September 25. Agnew, already plea-bargaining with Attorney General Elliot Richardson, demands that the House initiate "a full inquiry."

September 26. House Speaker Carl Albert denies Agnew's request, a decision Ford labels both "political" and "unfortunate."

October 5. The Justice Department argues that a sitting vice president may be indicted --but offers the House the opportunity to impeach him first.

October 6. Egypt and Syria attack Israel and begin the Yom Kippur War.

October 10. Agnew resigns and pleads no contest to a single charge of income tax evasion. Ford's reaction: "You're kidding'."

October 11. Leading Republicans send Nixon their preferential list of vice presidential candidates. Ford emerges as the choice of Congress.

October 12. Circuit Court of Appeals orders Nixon to release five more Watergate tapes.

At 7:30 P.M., Alexander Haig informs Ford he is to be nominated. At 9:00 P.M., Nixon introduces Ford on national television as "man who has earned the respect of both Democrats and Republicans." Ford is the first vice president nominated under terms of the 25th Amendment.

October 13. The New York Times terms Ford, Nixon's
"easy way out." Ford asserts "as emphatically and as
strongly as I can, I have no intention of being a candidate
for any office. . . in 1976."

October 15. Agnew's farewell speech declares Ford's nomination "wise;" he is "an eminently fair and capable individual . . . clearly qualified to undertake the highest
office."

October 20. In what is referred to as the Saturday Night
Massacre, Nixon dismisses Special Prosecutor Cox. Elliot
Richardson and Deputy Attorney General William Ruckel-
shaus resign, and a "firestorm" of outrage sweeps the nation. Governor Jimmy Carter (D-Ga.) says the firing is
"an act that warrants impeachment."

November 1. The Senate begins two weeks of hearings on
Ford's nomination. Although some witnesses denounce him
as a "final passage" man on civil rights/social legislation,
Senator Howard Cannon defends Nixon's right to have an
ideologically compatible vice president.

November 15. The House Judiciary Committee begins eleven
days of hearings. Ford is bluntly told he probably will soon
be president and says, "I don't think the public would stand
for" the pardon of an impeached president. His net worth,
as of September 30, 1973, is set at $256,378.

November 27. The Senate approves Ford by a vote of 92-
3.

December 6. House approval is voted, 387-35, although
Peter Rodino, Chairman of the Judiciary Committee, votes
nay on the basis of Ford's conservative record. Before a
Joint Session of Congress, Ford takes the oath as fortieth
vice president of the United States. His pledge of "full
support and loyalty" to Nixon is kept faithfully for the next
eight months.

December 7. Ford asserts that Nixon "has no intention of
resigning" and will be exonerated when all the facts become
known. He serves on both the Domestic Council and the
National Security Council.

December 8. Nixon asks the Congressional Joint Committee to decide if he owes up to $267,000 in back taxes.

December 12. Ford says he expects to see Nixon daily and describes his 1976 prospects "as close to a Shermanesque statement as you can get." Advised by Goodell, he begins to travel widely, speaks "affirmatively" on foreign policy and steadfastly refuses to listen to any tapes.

1974   January 15. Ford addresses the American Farm Bureau Congress with a speech written by the White House. Ignoring the Watergate indictments, he praises the president's philosophy and his foreign policy achievements. Impeachment talk is only "a massive propaganda campaign."

January 18. The fruits of Secretary Henry Kissinger's "shuttle diplomacy" become apparent as Israel and Egypt agree to a Suez disengagement.

February 3. Appearing on "Face the Nation," Ford agrees that all tapes and documents should be delivered to the House Judiciary Committee. However, before an Iowa audience, he calls Nixon "as good if not better than any President in the history of our country."

February 18. Democrat Richard VanderVeen wins a special election for Ford's congressional seat. His campaign called for a Nixon resignation that would "put Jerry in the White House." This Democratic win in the 5th Congressional District is their first there in sixty-four years, but Ford attributes the loss to a deteriorating economy and gasoline shortages.

April 30. Nixon releases edited transcripts of his Oval Office conversations. To many they show shocking amorality in the White House but Ford is only "a little disappointed." He remains "convinced beyond any doubt that the President is innocent."

May-July. Ford travels extensively defending Nixon. As vice president he visits forty states and logs 115,000 miles in eight months. His advisors, led by Philip Buchan and Clay Whitehead, begin to plan the transition to a Ford presidency.

May 9. The House Judiciary Committee begins impeachment hearings.

May 31. An Israeli-Syrian disengagement is announced by
Kissinger.

June. At Michigan University's graduation, Ford calls Mao
Tse-tung "one of the great world leaders" and urges Amer-
ca's youth to emulate that of China.

July 24. The Supreme Court orders the president to produce sixty-four White House tapes. Ford asserts "from
the bottom of my heart that the president of the United
States is innocent. He is right."

July 27-30. The House Judiciary Committee votes three
counts of impeachment against Richard Nixon.

THE ACCIDENTAL PRESIDENT

August 1. Haig, de facto acting president, tells Ford of
the "smoking gun" in the new tapes to be released which
will doom Nixon's cause. Ford, who cannot appear to do
anything toward forcing a resignation, refuses to make
any response.

August 3-5. Ford continues to defend the president on his
last vice presidential trip. On August 6, he consults with
Buchan on transition plans.

August 7. Hartmann begins to draft Ford's acceptance
speech, and Haig informs Ford he is certain to be president.

August 8. Ford meets with Nixon at 11:00 A.M. Nixon resigns in an evening speech over national television.

August 9. At 11:35 A.M., while he is en route to California,
Nixon's resignation is delivered to Secretary of State Kissinger. At that instant, Gerald R. Ford became 38th president of the United States; the oath was administered at 12:03
P.M. by Chief Justice Warren Burger. Ford tells America

that "our long national nightmare is over" and takes control of a shocked land. Inflation is at 12.2 per cent, unemployment at 5.3 per cent and the Dow Jones Index at 784.89.

Jerald terHorst is named press secretary.

August 10. All cabinet and agency heads are asked to remain in office because "that is what the country wants". " Ford solicits vice presidential nominations and has our Moscow ambassador assure Leonid Brezhnev of continued personal diplomacy toward detente.

August 11. Ford signs his first two bills and meets with the Israeli foreign minister.

August 12. In "the people's House, " Ford addresses Congress and calls for "a good marriage." He asks greater fiscal restraint to curb inflation and endorses a "domestic summit" on the economy. His task will be to restore "trust" and he minds them [I am] "still a Ford, but I am not a Model T. "

August 13. Ford asks George Meany, of the AFL-CIO, to cooperate in the fight against inflation.

August 14. Another "firestorm" erupts when the White House declares Nixon's tapes and papers are personal property that must revert to his exclusive control.

Ford signs a bill that allows Americans to purchase gold after January 1.

August 16. All Nixon tapes will be held in the White House until the legal problems of Watergate are resolved. Ford names Philip Buchan his counsel. A battle between old Nixon staffers and new Ford men takes place for the rest of the summer.

August 17. The White House explicitly denies that Nelson Rockefeller, ex-governor of New York, has any ties to 1972 campaign "dirty tricks" and indicates he remains "under consideration" for the vice presidency.

August 19. Ford's first presidential trip is to address the V.F.W. Convention in Chicago. He endorses "leniency" for draft evaders and favors "earned re-entry" into American life.

In Cyprus, the American ambassador is shot to death.

August 20. Ford nominates Nelson Rockefeller, "a good partner for me, " to be vice president.

August 21. Ford will "probably" be a candidate for president in 1976 -- the only real surprise is the speed of his announcement. In a flurry of activity designed to show "business as usual", he signs a $25 billion education bill at HEW Headquarters, pressures General Motors into price rollbacks and fulfills an invitation extended on August 12 by meeting with the Congressional Black Caucus.

August 22. Ford announces his support for the Equal Rights Amendment.

August 23. The day after the House Judiciary Committee publishes a 528 page report on Nixon's impeachment proceedings, vice presidential designee Rockefeller asserts the former president should not be prosecuted. Ford permits former Nixon aides access to White House files.

August 24. Ford signs legislation creating the Council on Wage and Price Stability --he reiterates his opposition to wage/price controls and asserts he will limit spending in fiscal 1975 (ending June 30, 1975) to $300 billion.

August 26. The Gallup Poll finds that 71 per cent of Americans approve Ford's actions as president.

Meetings of administration and business leaders will precede the September 27-30 "summit conference" on America's economic condition.

August 28. A friendly mood pervades Ford's press conference, for which he rehearsed ten hours. The president asserts no budget will be "sacrosanct" in holding spending below $300 billion; he will follow Nixon's conservative social and economic policies. Ford declares, "I am the final authority" on pardoning Nixon, who has already been enormously punished by his forced resignation.

August 29. Ford asks Congress to approve $850,000 for Nixon's transition to private life. A bitter power struggle is being waged between Ford counselor Robert Hartmann and Nixon holdover Alexander Haig.

August 31. A day after a Pentagon study concludes a "substantial majority" of Americans want an amnesty program
for Vietnam draft evaders, Ford says he has some ideas
of his own on the proposals and will implement an executive program.

September 1. The president's Labor Day message urges
unions to increase their productivity in order to help America fight inflation. America's jobless rate is 5.4 per
cent and George Meany fears a national depression.

September 2. Ford signs the Employee Benefit Security
Act and the pension rights of 23 million Americans are
given federal protection.

September 3. General Creighton Abrams, commander of
U.S. forces in Vietnam, dies.

September 4. The United States opens diplomatic ties with
East Germany and John Sherman Cooper becomes the first
ambassador. George Bush is named envoy to Red China
while Kenneth Ruth, designated Cost of Living Council
chief on August 29, is nominated ambassador to France.

September 5. Ford opens the first of twelve regional economic conferences; he calls for a "battle plan against a common enemy, inflation." Administration economic advisors
believe only long-term fiscal and monetary restraint can
bring down inflation.

September 7. CIA Director William Colby testifies that
$8,000,000 was authorized for covert activities in Chile
from 1970-1973. Allegations of CIA complicity in the over-
throw of Salvador Allende bedevil the Ford administration
until December, 1975.

September 8. Ford grants "a full, free and absolute pardon
unto Richard Nixon," but his "act of mercy" causes public
outrage because Nixon admitted "mistakes" but no wrong-
doing. Public approval of Ford drops to 49 per cent,
according to Gallup, and Press Secretary terHorst
resigns in protest. The White House also announces
that Watergate tapes will ultimately be returned to Nixon.

September 11. The White House, in the wake of the "firestorm" of pardon protest, denies that Ford has any inten-

tion of pardoning forty-eight other Watergate figures.

September 12. Mayor Abraham Beame of New York says
his city is being destroyed by constantly increasing costs
and falling revenues.

Ford asks restoration of the $700,000,000 slashed from the
South Vietnam appropriation.

Violence mars court-ordered integration via busing in Boston.

September 13. The Dow Jones stock index hits a twelve year
low at 627.19; in Ford's first month in office that index lost
99 points while wholesale prices rose 3.9% in August.

September 14. Jerry terHorst, now a columnist, reveals
that Ford spends an "inordinate amount of time" dealing
with the feud between his loyalists and Alexander Haig. On
September 16, Ford names Haig to be commander of NATO,
a post he assumes December 15.

September 16. At a press conference Ford defends his pardon of Nixon, backs the CIA's clandestine work to "implement
foreign policy and protect national security" and announces a
clemency program which provides for "earned reentry" of
deserters into American life. He names Charles Goodell
chairman of a nine-member Clemency Board.

September 17. Nixon is ill with phlebitis and his lawyers announce he cannot testify at the Watergate trial of Haldeman
and Ehrlichman. The House cuts his proposed transition
budget.

September 18. Addressing the U.N. General Assembly,
Ford proposes "a global strategy for food and energy." He
pledges his "full support and the unquestioned backing of the
American people" to Secretary of State Kissinger, who is
conceded to be operating American foreign policy.

September 19. Ford is "disappointed" when the Senate orders
pay raises for 3,600,000 federal employees on October 1
instead of January 1; their largesse increases the budget by
$700,000,000.

September 21. Ford meets Russian Ambassador Gromyko
and concludes two days of discussion on the Mid-East, arms

limitations and detente. Gromyko praises detente in his
speech to the United Nations on September 24.

September 23. In the wake of a quadrupling of oil prices
by the OPEC cartel, Ford and Kissinger warn of depression
and a "breakdown of world order."

Senator Edward Kennedy removes himself from the 1976
presidential race: "I simply cannot do that to my wife and
children and the other members of my family."

September 24. The House, by a vote of 309-90, halts arms
aid to Turkey pending progress toward a Cyprus solution.

The Senate Government Operation Committee unanimously
voids Ford's plan for Nixon's tapes and papers.

September 25. A record trade deficit of $1.1 billion for the
month of August is announced.

Brezhnev lauds detente and says he would be happy to visit
America in 1975.

September 26. The Shah of Iran rejects Ford's appeal for
lower oil prices "No one can dictate to us."

Donald Rumsfeld begins to act as White House Chief of Staff.

September 27. A two-day economic summit convenes as the
market hits another twelve year low. Ford labels inflation
"Public Enemy Number One" and designates Secretary
William Simon to coordinate efforts to bring it under control.

September 28. Mrs. Elizabeth "Betty" Ford undergoes a
mastectomy.

September 30. The Senate by a vote of 57-20 cuts arms aid
to Turkey.

Ford offers to personally testify before the House of Judiciary Committee and explain his pardon of Nixon.

October 1. The Senate sets a tone of confrontation with the
executive when it reaffirms its Turkish arms ban, cuts off
military aid of Chile and halts fertilizer exports to South

Vietnam.

October 2. The House slashes Nixon's transition funds to
$200,000.

October 3. Ford wins a major victory over Congress when
a conference committee removes the ban on aid to Turkey
and Chile.

The House completes action on the six year, $11 billion,
Mass Transit bill.

October 4. The administration halts a 125 bushel grain sale
to the Soviet Union in order to reduce domestic inflation.

The Senate, 56-7, orders an end to Ford's tape/paper agreement with Nixon; the former president leaves the hospital after twelve days of treatment for phlebitis.

October 5. Rockefeller, whose admitted wealth is $218
million, announces he made monetary gifts (up to $550,000
in one case) to politicians whose loyalty, personal friendship and services he admired.

October 7. The Senate formally ends the national emergen-
cies of 1933, 1950, 1970, 1971 in a move to limit executive
power. The House over-rides its Conference Committee
and insists on an end to aid to Turkey.

October 8. Ford exhorts America to "Whip Inflation Now
--WIN" and suggests a five per cent surcharge on all incomes over $15,000. He asks Americans to drive five per
cent less in order to reduce our dependence on foreign oil.
An enthusiastic stock market soars 28.39 points on October 9.

The Franklin National Bank announces insolvency and becomes the nation's largest bank failure.

October 9. In the wake of pupil violence in Boston, Ford
condemns the court's desegregation order; he has consistently opposed forced bussing of students.

October 11. Ford accepts resignations from J. Fred
Buzhardt and Patrick Buchanan as the new administration
slowly divests itself of Nixon appointees.

The Northrop Corporation admits a slush fund of $1,200,000 for political payoffs.

October 12. Leon Jaworski resigns as Special Watergate Prosecutor -- he did not oppose the Ford pardon of Nixon.

Kissinger predicts international "interdependence," or else "Western civilization . . . is almost certain to disintegrate."

October 14. Ford vetoes the appropriation bill that halts arms aid to Turkey.

The U.N. General Assembly votes (105-4) to allow the Palestinian Liberation Organization to participate in its Mid-Eastern deliberations.

October 15. Rockefeller, angry at publicity given his gifts, asks immediate congressional consideration of his nomination lest he be "tried in the press."

The House fails to override Ford's veto of the Turkish aid prohibition, and approves extention of the cut-off date to December 10.

Ford calls on Americans to voluntarily act against inflation . The economy is statistically in a recession but the administration will not admit this fact.

October 16. The president tours the Midwest campaigning for fiscally conservative Republicans; he warns of "legislative dictatorship" if Democrats sweep the November elections. In North Carolina (October 19) he asks Americans to prevent a "veto-proof" Congress.

October 17. Ford appears before the House Judiciary Committee to deny allegations of a "deal" on the Nixon pardon. His motive was "to serve the best interests of my country."

Ford vetoes the Freedom of Information Act, but Congress overides the veto.

October 18. Senator Henry Jackson announces that trade legislation with the Soviet Union will depend on its guarantees of Jewish emigration rights.

A $3 billion housing act is signed by the president.

October 19. The administration approves a reduced $380 million grain deal with Russia.

October 21. Ford confers in New Mexico with Mexican President Luis Echeverria.

The Federal Court orders a delay in Ford's arrangement with Nixon regarding presidential papers.

October 23. The White House withdraws Ford's campaign remarks about Democrats; "he didn't intend to say that Democrats are a party of war."

October 25. Ford pledges to black leaders that he will fully enforce all civil rights laws.

October 26. Kissinger completes three days of Moscow talks which set up an arms control summit between Ford and Brezhnev.

Henry S. Ruth becomes Watergate prosecutor.

October 28. At Rabat, the Arab states unanimously endorse creation of an independent Palestinian state on lands to be "liberated" from Israel. To Kissinger, such a declaration will not hinder Mid-Eastern progress (October 30).

October 29. Despite nine vetoes, Ford's "marriage" with Congress is still good. The president forces the resignation of energy "czar" William Sawhill, who favored higher gasoline taxes. His "new team" is led by Secretary of Interior Rogers Morton.

October 30. The United States joins with Britain and France to veto the U.N.'s expulsion of South Africa.

October 31. Despite transfer of three generals, students continue to protest the regime of South Vietnam's President Nguyen Van Thieu.

November 1. Turkish resettlement of captured areas in northern Cyprus de facto creates an ethnic province.

Ford spends eight minutes with Nixon, who is recovering from phlebitis surgery.

November 2. Ford completes 16, 685 miles of campaigning in twenty states for Republicans. He asks for a large
vote to help him govern effectively but unemployment in
October is six per cent and anger at his pardon of
Nixon remains extremely high.

November 5. The Democrats win 290 seats in the House.
No House candidate that Ford campaigned for wins and in
Michigan's Fifth C.D., VanderVeen maintains his seat.
Democrats gain in House, Senate, and gubernatorial races.

November 6. Revelations about Andrew Gibson's oil interests imperil his appointment as federal energy adminis-
trator; the nomination is withdrawn at his request on November 12.

November 7. At the World Food Conference in Rome, Earl
Butz agrees to United States participation in a program
where major world grain producers will foreign sales in
order to supply more grain to the world's hungry people.
Ford, however, on November 15, refuses to commit America to a million ton emergency food increase.

November 8. Edward Morgan admits backdating documents
to obtain fraudulent tax deductions for Nixon.

Secretary of the Army Howard "Bo" Callaway announces the
parole of William Calley, the only officer convicted of the
Mylai massacre in Vietnam.

November 9. Ford pays $435.77 in an IRS disallowed de-
duction on his 1972 income tax.

November 10. A national coal miners strike begins in West
Virginia.

Senator Robert Dole advises Ford to "toughen up" if he intends to win the presidency in 1976.

November 11. Ford's WIN "Citizens Action Committee"
calls for voluntary action against inflation -- the campaign
fails abysmally and is officially ended on March 8, 1975.

All Nixon tapes and documents are placed under the control
of Special Prosecutor Ruth.

November 12. Press Secretary Ron Nessen concedes that
the U.S. is moving into recession.

South Africa is suspended from participation in the U.N.
General Assembly.

November 13. Yasir Arafat of the Palestinian Liberation
Organization addresses the U.N.: "I have come bearing
an olive branch and a freedom fighter's gun."

November 14. Ford personally rebukes Army Chief George Brown for remarks at Duke University which suggested
Jewish control of American news media. He also demands
that Congress "fish or cut bait" on his nomination of Rockefeller to be vice president.

November 16. Ford imposes a quota on Canadian beef and
pork imports.

Interior Secretary Morton "gets the word" from Ford --
there are to be no higher gasoline taxes.

November 17. Ford leaves the United States for a trip to
Japan, South Korea, and Vladivostok, Russia.

November 19. Ford meets with Emperor Hirohito and Prime
Minister Tanaka of Japan.

November 21. The Senate approves the Mass Transit Bill.

UNESCO votes to exclude Israel from its European group.

November 23. After a stopover in Korea, Ford arrives in
Vladivostok to meet with Premier Brezhnev. On November
24 they agree to limit strategic missiles to 2400, of which
1320 may be MIRVed.

Representative Morris Udall becomes the first Democrat to
announce his candidacy for the presidency.

November 25. Frank Zarb is named federal energy admin-
istrator.

November 26. Ford signs the $11.8 billion mass transit bill.
He admits FY75s budget cannot be held below $300 billion,
but asks Congress for fiscal restraint. To illustrate his own

commitment, he vetoes a veterans education bill.

November 27. Gallup reports Ford's approval rating falls to forty-seven per cent.

The U.N. seat of the Cambodian government of General Lol Nol is maintained due to U.S. pressure; the vote is 56-54.

November 29. A three-doctor panel agrees Nixon is too ill to testify at the Watergate cover-up trial and he is excused from appearing.

Ford rebukes Secretary Butz who mocked Pope Paul's opposition to birth control. Butz publicly apologizes.

December 2. Despite Ford's professed desire for merit appointments, a secret White House memo asks federal agencies to give the "best possible exposure" to defeated/retiring Republican congressmen and their staffs.

Ford asserts the Vladivostok talks put a "firm ceiling" on the arms race but America still faces three crises: inflation, recession and energy.

Pioneer II transmits pictures of the polar area of Jupiter.

December 3. Both the House (394-10) and Senate (90-1) override Ford's veteran education veto. Ford's "honeymoon" with Congress is over after fifteen vetoes and a "growing sense of frustration" with congressional spending is apparent at the White House.

December 4. The Democratic caucus decides to weaken seniority rights, end dual chairmanships, and remove committee assignments from the Ways and Means Committee.

December 5. Intervention by Secretary of the Treasury Simon ends a twenty-four day strike and obtains a three year contract for the coal industry.

December 6. Ford concedes the failure of his energy conservation program. The Democratic Party, meeting in a non-presidential convention, condemns Ford's "callous economic nonsense."

Ambassador John Scali attacks the "tyranny of the majority" in the U.N. General Assembly.

December 9. Henry Ford calls on Ford to create a "sub-
stantive" program to avert economic chaos. New car sales
have dropped by a third and unemployment is 6.5 per cent,
its highest level since October, 1961.

December 10. The Senate approves the Rockefeller nomination, 90-7.

December 11. Speaking to business leaders, Ford concedes
"the economy is in difficult straits" but indicates he will
not change 180 degrees from inflation fighting to pump-prim-
ing.

December 12. Jimmy Carter becomes the second Democrat
to announce his candidacy for the 1976 presidential nomination.

December 13. The Senate completes twenty months of effort and approves, 77-4, a trade bill offering economic concessions to Russia in return for freer emigration policies
(especially for Jews).

The resignation of Attorney General William Saxbe is announced. He is nominated ambassador to India while his
cabinet colleague Richardson will go to London's Court of
St. James.

December 15. Ford meets with French President Valery
Giscard d'Estaing on Martinique. They do not get on well
and, despite an agreement to coordinate energy policies,
France later decides to make its own oil agreement with
OPEC.

December 17. Roy Ash resigns as head of OMB -- his last
project is the FY76 budget, which he prepares with his successor, James Lynn.

December 18. Russia denies it agreed to trade Jewish emigration rights for increased commerce. Secretary Kissinger was informed of this position by letter on October 25.

December 19. The House confirms Rockefeller, 287-128, and
he is sworn in as America's forty-first vice president. In

retrospect, due to right-wing Republican antipathy to Rockefeller, the nomination may have been a crucial blunder.

December 20. Congress adjourns after sending the Russian trade bill to Ford. Jewish leaders urge him not to use
his tariff cutting authority unless the right of emigration is
assured.

December 22. Domestic intelligence operations by the CIA
are revealed in the Times and the exposure begins a year
of revelations against intelligence agencies. Ford had "partial knowledge" of the program as vice president but now
explicitly orders the CIA not to engage in any operation
within the United States. CIA Director Colby flies on December 24 to Vail, Colorado, where the president is vaca-
tioning, and confirms the essentials of the story.

December 23. The B-1 bomber prototype makes its first
flight.

Ford vetoes bills to expand federal health services and pollution control progress. He is gratified when U.S. Steel
reduces announced price rises by twenty per cent due to
administration pressure.

December 25. A man dressed as an Arab crashes through
the White House gates and delays his capture for four hours
by threatening to explode a non-existent bomb.

December 27. Ford signs a bill that provides $200,000
for Nixon's transition costs, but which prohibits transfer
of his presidential papers and tapes to California. Nixon
lawyers file suit in August 1975 to order their return.

December 28. In a year-end interview Ford reveals his
intention to establish a special panel to deal with the CIA
revelations; many top-level "spooks" soon resign.

December 30. Ford pocket vetoes the strip mining bill despite strong objections from environmentalists. Since taking office, he has vetoed twenty bills and has had three over-
ridden.

December 31. The Nixon Foundation announces that it will
not construct a separate Nixon Library.

Ford signs the Public Service Employment Bill

FORD ON HIS OWN

1975   January 1. John Mitchell, H. R. Haldeman, John Ehrlichman, and Robert Mardian are convicted for perjury and conspiracy to obstruct justice in the Watergate case. Nixon is reportedly "anguished" by the verdict.

Justice Douglas suffers a severe stroke.

January 2. The recession deepens as December unemployment reaches 7.1 per cent, and Ford decides to make the 180 degree turn he denounced on December 11. Commerce Department figures indicate that the last quarter of 1974 had the greatest decline in industrial production since 1958.

January 3. Ford signs into law the most sweeping Trade Act in 40 years; however, its provisions for trade with Soviet Russia are cancelled January 14, due to the Jewish emigration issue.

A "highly inflationary" milk price-support bill is vetoed by the president.

January 4. Ford signs the $4.5 billion appropriation to extend unemployment insurance benefits.

January 5. Rockefeller is named to lead the "Blue Ribbon" investigation of the CIA.

January 7. Phouc Binh falls to the North Vietnamese, the first South Vietnamese capitol to be captured since May, 1972. This defeat signals the beginning of the end of America's presence in Vietnam, although the president asks Congress to appropriate an additional $300,000,000 in military aid.

January 8. The Watergate-related sentences of John Dean, Herbert Kalmbach and Jeb Magruder are commuted to time already served.

January 10. The Ford Motor Company announces that twenty-two of its plants will close for a week.

January 11. Senator Kennedy accuses Ford of ignoring court decisions in a "desperate gamble to hang onto the pocket veto power."

January 12. Kissinger's controversial suggestion that the U.S. might someday use force in the Middle East win's Ford's approval; it could only occur if an oil embargo caused "actual strangulation of the industrial world."

January 13. Ford goes on national television to reverse his economic policies. Calling for a "three front campaign against recession, inflation and energy dependence," he proposes a $16 billion tax cut and higher gasoline taxes. The program gets only tepid business support and is rejected by congressional Democrats.

January 14. Ford announces he will nominate Edward Levi as attorney general and William Coleman as secretary of transportation. They are easily confirmed.

The United States, denouncing North Vietnam's "flagrant violations" of the Paris cease-fire, asserts its own freedom to violate the agreements.

January 15. The president declares that the State of the Union is "not good," and proposes tax cuts, public job programs, and removal of the ceiling on oil prices. The latter precipitates a year long battle with Congress.

January 18. Ford's public endorsement of Secretary Simon averts his resignation over the philosophic issues of tax cuts and deficits.

In Cambodia, Khymer Rouge rebels complete the isolation of Phnom Penh while in Cyprus 5,000 youths burn part of the U.S. Embassy.

January 20. The S nate votes to establish a select committee, ultimately led by Frank Church, to investigate the CIA.

General Motors joins Chrysler and Ford in announcing rebates for new auto sales, which declined 24 per cent in 1974.

Chou En-lai of China says war between the U.S. and the USSR is "inevitable."

January 21. Ford announces he will veto any mandatory gasoline rationing as "inequitable."

January 22. House Democrats complete overhaul of their committee structure by ousting three chairmen and severely revising the seniority system.

International agreements banning chemical and biological warfare are signed by the president.

January 23. A presidential proclamation imposes an additional one dollar fee on each barrel of oil imported after February 1; additional dollars will be levied on March 1 and April 1.

Ford tells NBC News that he is "very secure" in the presidency; "my feeling of certainty grows every day."

January 26. Representatives of OPEC complete three days of talks in Algiers and condemn U.S. threats toward their cartel. The U.S. trade deficit for 1974 was over $3 billion largely due to oil import prices.

January 28. The "Weather Underground" explodes a bomb at the State Department to protest U.S. aid to Vietnam. Ford asks a reluctant Congress to appropriate another half billion dollars in new military aid for Southeast Asia.

January 29. Ford orders implementation of the Vladivostok arms limitation agreement.

The House authorizes a bipartisan investigation of intelligence activities and abuses.

January 30. The president's amnesty program is extended to March 1.

January 31. The Federal District Court rules that the government and not Richard Nixon owns the 42,000,000 items comprising his presidential papers. Judge Charles Richey also decides that claims to executive privilege end when a president leaves office.

February 1. Secretary Kissinger fails to obtain congressional approval for arms sales to Turkey beyond February 4. In the Mideast, despite a loan offer of $25,000,000 to Syria, his shuttle diplomacy has stalled. This winter is the nadir of his policy as SALT and detente are being criticized, Vietnam and Portugal seem about to go Communist, and CIA revelations continue.

February 2. Chairman Albert Ullman of the House Ways and Means Committee announces he will seek a tax cut of $22 billion; he calls Ford's oil import reduction plan "unrealistic."

February 4. Ford sends a budget message to Congress which forecasts average unemployment of 8.1 per cent and inflation of 11.3 per cent in 1975. The first figure proves too low, the second too high, but Representative Sam Gibbons of Florida expresses a common reaction: "he's going to be a two year president."

February 5. The Senate rejects the administration's reduced food stamp program and orders an investigation of abuses.

The House votes to suspend for ninety days the president's right to increase fees on imported oil. To the White House all Congress does on energy is to "vote for delay."

Over 100,000 UAW members rally in Washington demanding government action against the recession.

February 6. Secretary of Labor Peter Brennan resigns. His successor will be Professor John Dunlop of Harvard.

February 9. Kissinger leaves Washington for another Mideast "shuttle."

Nixon's six month transition period ends but his shadow always haunts the Ford presidency.

February 10. While visiting Texas, Ford continues his attacks on congressional inaction in the fields of energy and economics. January industrial output fell another 3.8 per cent while unemployment reaches 8.2 per cent.

February 11. The president releases $2 billion in impounded highway funds to stimulate economic recovery -- the money must be spent by June 30.

February 13. Ford announces he will name Carla Hills to be Secretary of Housing and Urban Development. Only the third woman to serve in a cabinet, she is sworn in on March 10.

Turkey proclaims a separate state now exists in northern occupied Cyprus.

February 14. Cambodian troops fail to reopen the Mekong River to Phnom Penh.

February 15. Elmer Klassen resigns as head of the postal service and is replaced by Benjamin Bailar.

February 16. The Ford administration approves Iran's $300,000,000 investment in Pan American Airlines, but the deal ultimately fails to materialize.

Senator Jesse Helms launches a study of a Conservative third party, an idea denounced by the administration.

February 18. The governors of New York, New Jersey, and Connecticut charge that Ford's economic policies accept "planned unemployment" and fail to act in the face of "depression."

February 19. The Senate concurs with the House and approves a delay in oil import fees for ninety days. Ford "regrets" the legislation and will veto the measure.

February 20. CIA Director Colby charges that "exaggerated" charges about CIA activities have "placed American intelligence in danger."

February 21. The Watergate conspirators are sentenced and immediately announce their appeals.

A touring Russian trade official questions America's ability to honor its agreements in light of the failure of the trade accord.

February 23. Secretary of Defense James Schlesinger blames Congress for condoning a "foreign policy disaster;" without additional aid of $222,000,000 Cambodia will fall.

February 24. The United States lifts its ten year embargo on arms shipments to Pakistan.

Ford proposes railroad consolidation plans for seventeen northeastern states -- a 15000 mile system will be created.

February 25. The stock market experiences its sharpest break since November 18, 1974 -- stocks drop almost eightteen points to 719.18.

February 25. Ford denounces the Arab boycott of 1500 firms that deal with Israel; "such discrimination is totally contrary to the American tradition and repugnant to American principles."

February 27. By a vote of 317-97, the House approves a $21.3 billion tax cut measure that also repeals the oil depletion allowance.

Attorney General Levi confirms that J. Edgar Hoover kept secret files on government officials and allowed the Agency to be improperly utilized for political purposes.

February 28. Recession strikes America hard with February unemployment 8.2 per cent, farm prices down for the fourth month and industrial prices down for the fifth consecutive month. Despite these figures, Ford "undoubtedly" will enter the 1976 presidential race.

Goodell praises as "a bonus" the president's extension of the Clemency Board until March 31.

March 1. Sixty-two protestors are arrested at the White House as they denounce "shamnesty" and the military aid program.

USDA reports discover $160,000,000 in food stamp overpayments, yet the next day the Senate Committee on Nutrition reveals that only 38 per cent of eligible Americans applied for help.

March 3. Graham Martin, U.S. Ambassador to Saigon, arrives in Washington to personally lobby for military aid.

The administration requests a reduced school lunch program that will save $4 billion in five years.

March 4. Ford vetoes the ninety day delay in oil import tariffs, but delays imposing the dollar fee scheduled for March while he seeks a compromise with Congress.

Iran signs a $15 billion economic aid pact with the United States.

March 5. The CIA admits it opened the mail of Representative Bella Abzug (D-NY). The president declines a request from the Senate Select Committe on Intelligence that he order agencies to cooperate with their investigators; rather, informational requests will be handled on a "case by case" basis.

The Senate, 73-21, eases its filibuster rules and ultimately allows sixty votes to achieve cloture.

March 6. At his nationally televised press conference, the president demands Congress act on his Asian aid requests so no power will question the "reliability" of the United States.

March 8. Ronald Reagan, former governor of California, rejects Ford's appeal for a broader GOP -- "a political party cannot be all things to all people. " -- and signals his intention of challenging Ford for the Republican nomination.

The FBI admits a campaign of harassment against Martin Luther King, a program which included mailing "unsavory" tapes on King's personal life to his wife.

March 9. Construction begins on a 789 mile, 43 inch wide, pipeline to deliver Alaskan oil to the "lower 48."

Iraq attacks its Kurdish minority with the tacit approval of both Secretary Kissinger and Iran; the Kurds are crushed in two weeks.

March 10-17. John Hersey spends a week with Ford; his observations are reported in the Times and are the basis for The President (1975).

March 11. The SEC accuses Gulf Oil of making $10,000,000 in illegal political contributions since 1960.

The Common Market offers easier terms to keep Britain a member.

March 12. The House, 189-49, rejects additional aid to Cambodia and South Vietnam.

Former Secretary of Commerce Maurice Stans becomes Nixon's third cabinet officer found guilty of a crime. He admits five fund raising law violations during the 1972 campaign and is fined $5, 000.

March 15. Portugal's left wing government, having crushed an abortive coup, completes the nationalization of its banks and insurance companies.

March 17. In South Vietnam, President Thieu orders the evacuation of the Central Highlands. The unexpected decision precipitates a rout that causes the fall of his regime. At a press conference Ford claims the fall of Cambodia "could vitally affect the national security of the United States, " and affirms his belief in the domino theory. He condemns all past CIA assassination plots against foreign leaders.

March 18. A successful CIA operation is revealed in the New York Times; the agency raised a sunken Soviet nuclear submarine.

The House, 333-86, joins the Senate, which voted on March 12, in approving a new Strip Mining Bill.

March 19. Quang Tri falls in South Vietnam. The disaster is due partly to lack of U.S. aid, says General George Brown, an opinion Ford echoes on March 20.

March 20. Justice Douglas returns to the Supreme Court for the first time since his stroke.

March 21. The Senate, by a vote of 60-29, approves a tax cut of $29. 2 billion which maintains the oil depletion allowance for smaller companies.

March 23. Kissinger completes a Mid-eastern "shuttle" which has been operative since March 8; his talks apparently fail over Israel's demand for an Arab pledge of non-belligerency. The president, angered at Israel's intransigence, orders a "review" of U.S. policy in that area of the world.

March 24. The Dow plunges to 743.43 in light of America's Mideastern and Asian debacles.

March 25. Faisal of Saudi Arabia is assassinated and his brother Khalid becomes king.

March 26. Congress completes a $22.8 billion tax cut bill, a measure providing for individual rebates, higher deductions, investment tax credit and an end to oil depletion allowances for large companies.

Kissinger denounces Congress for "selective reliability" and proposes a three-year Saigon aid program.

March 29. An unhappy Ford signs the tax bill; it was "take it or leave it."

Danang falls to the North Vietnamese. During the rout, ARVIN forces have abandoned a billion dollars of equipment and preyed on refugeees.

Federal Court rules constitutional Ford's pardon of Nixon.

March 31. The clemency program ends. Of 106.472 eligible men, only 21,723 applied for pardons. Goodell calls the effort "reasonable and successful."

As the siege of Phnom Penh tightens, President Lol Nol leaves for exile.

Industrial production fell by 28.4 per cent in the first quarter of 1975, a post war record. Agricultural products continued to fall in March and unemployment leaped to 8.7 per cent. Only 39 per cent of Americans polled by Gallup professed confidence in Ford.

April 1. The American Freedom Train begins a twenty-one month, eighty city tour in celebration of the American Bicentennial.

April 2. New York City's credit rating is downgraded by Standard and Poor, but not by Moody's. The city has already appealed to Ford (March 21-23) for "massive" aid to meet its cash flow problems since it cannot market short term notes.

April 3. After a week's tour of Vietnam, Army Chief of
Staff Frederick Weyland asserts "capability" to win is still
present. The president says the U.S. will honor its committments and berates congressional inaction. He tells
them to "stop coming to the White House with one spending
bill after another."

April 5. In San Diego, Ford personally meets a plane carrying evacuated children from South Vietnam. The previous day, a similar jet crashed, killing almost 200.

Chiang Kai-shek dies in Taiwan.

April 7. Senator Mike Mansfield, speaking for Congress,
rejects administration contentions that Congress is in any
way responsible for the loss of Indo-China.

The National Council on the Aging attacks Ford for placing
the heaviest economic burdens "on those who are most vulnerable: the elderly poor."

April 9. The SEC charges that United Brands Corp. paid
a $1,250,000 bribe to the president of Honduras. The ex-
ecutive responsible, Eli Black, committed suicide on February 3, and on April 22, Honduras overthrows its government.

The House of Commons approves continued British membership in the Common Market.

April 10. Ford asks a joint session of Congress for almost
a billion dollars in new aid to South Vietnam.

April 12. The United States closes its embassy in Phnom
Penh. In Saigon, military aides fear riots against Americans if evacuation begins.

April 13. Reports show that America has become the world's
greatest arms merchant, selling over $8 billion in mili-
tary equipment each year.

A busload of Palestinians is massacred by right-wing Christians in Lebanon -- the incident precipitates a twenty-one
month civil war.

April 14. The Senate's Foreign Relations Committee warns Ford not to use American troops to guard or to effect the evacuation of South Vietnam's leaders.

April 15. In a speech before the DAR, Ford asserts he will win the presidency in 1976. America must honor its committments to prevent the world power balance from shifting away from the United States: "To weaken our defenses is to weaken the foundation of detente."

April 16. Ford charges that America has failed in its committment to South Vietnam; in Cambodia, Phnom Penh surrenders.

The SEC accuses Northrop Corp. of maintaining a secret political payoff fund of $30,000,000; the company immediately agrees to a settlement.

April 17. Former Secretary of the Treasury John Connally is acquitted of bribery charges.

April 18. The president opens the bicentennial celebration in Boston by calling for a return to "basic American virtues."

April 19. As Communist troops complete the isolation of Saigon, Ford addresses a crowd at Concord. "Now is the time for reconciliation, not recrimination. It is a time for reconstruction -- not rancor."

April 20. Daniel Patrick Moynihan is selected our new ambassador to the United Nations and is sworn in by the president on June 30.

April 21. President Thieu resigns; his valedictory statement condemns America as "trustworthy."

In a CBS interview, Ford labels Israel "shortsighted" for opposing Mideastern compromise.

April 22. The president wins a six month struggle with the Senate when Thomas Meskill wins appointment to the Court of Appeals.

April 23. At Tulane University, Ford asserts the American role in Vietnam is over and we must cease "refighting

a war that is finished." Congress allows the use of troops
to evacuate American and South Vietnamese civilians,
while immigration restrictions are waived for new Asian
refugees.

April 24. Rockefeller, whose rulings helped Senate liberals reduce the power of the filibuster, admits a parliamen-
tary error and apologizes to Senator James Allen for any
unintended "discourtesy."

Congress passes legislation to reorganize federal super-
vision of the securities industry.

April 25. At Yale Law School, alumnus Ford says those
convicted of "violent crime should be sent to prison. . .
especially if a gun was involved." The president always
takes a hardline on crime.

The Senate passes a $6.1 billion public service jobs mea-
sure.

April 26. Despite Kissinger's apprehensions, Portuguese
moderates defeat Communists and win control of their
constituent assembly.

April 28. The United States withdraws its last personnel
from Saigon in a chaotic scene that sees two Marines die.
Ford comments that it is absurd to believe "if we do not
succeed in everything everywhere, then we have succeeded
in nothing anywhere."

The House passes a $3 billion school lunch bill, a billion
dollars over Ford's request.

Ford's economic advisor Allan Greenspan tells a New
York audience the recession will get worse -- just as the
economy begins its upturn. May is statistically the turning
point of the worst American economic recession since the
1930's.

April 29. The United States and Greece jointly announce
the closing of an Air Force base in Athens and also that
Eleusis will no longer serve as a home port for the Sixth
Fleet.

April 30. Saigon formally surrenders to the Communists
and thirty years of civil war come to a close. The widely

predicted "bloodbath" does not take place.

Ford once again defers imposing an additional fee on imported crude oil.

May 1. Ford vetoes the Farm Bill in order to hold his budget deficit below $60 billion.

The House refuses to vote a full $327,000,000 for refugee
aid as a wave of anti-Vietnamese anger sweeps the nation.
Ford will order a rise in refugee admissions to 123,000.

May 5. The United States recovers the most serviceable
of 120 planes which ferried Vietnamese refugees to Thailand. Reports indicate that the Khymer Rouge victory in
Cambodia has been followed by forced evacuation of its urban centers, a "march of death" for thousands.

May 6. The president uses a national press conference
to affirm American steadfastedness to its committments
and to assert that 50,000 Americans did not die in vain in
Vietnam. He is "damned mad" at unthinking animosity towards refugees and appeals to the nation to welcome the
newcomers as we did the Hungarians and Cubans.

May 7. Ford begins a month-long series of conferences
with America's allies in both Asia and Europe -- a compaign designed to reassure them of American support.

May 9. Congressional conferees approve a spending ceiling of $367 billion for fiscal 1976 with a deficit of $68.8
billion -- both levels far beyond Ford's limit of $355 and
$60 billion.

May 10. Secretary William Simon denies government monetary help to New York City; "the fundamental solution
to the city's financial problems does not lie at the federal
level." Mayor Beame bitterly charges that the Lockheed
loan indicates Republican bias toward business and against
cities.

May 12-15. An international crisis erupts when Cambodia
seizes the Mayaguez, a U.S. merchant ship travelling in
international waters. Ford considers this "an act of pira-
cy" and when the ship and its crew are not immediately
released he orders an attack by U.S. Marines. The crew

was released before the assault began and air attacks continued even after their safety was known. Ford did not consult Congress yet got its complete support. To save a freed crew of thirty-nine the nation suffered forty-one dead
and fifty injured but the president's favorable rating in the
polls leaps from 39 per cent to 51 per cent.

May 13. The House, due to the defection of urban Democrats, sustains the Farm Bill veto by 245-182.

May 14-15. Ford personally writes to New York's Mayor
Beame refusing to support a program of federal loans.
Simon asserts the impact of a New York City default would
be "negligible."

May 16. Gulf Oil Corp. admits over $5,000,000 in illegal
foreign bribes.

The reaction to Mayaguez includes student riots in Laos;
the withdrawal of the Thai ambassador in Washington;
Kissinger's avowal, "there are limits beyond which the
United States cannot be pushed."

May 18. The administration moves to foster competition
in railroads, trucking and air travel by proposing measures to reduce federal controls in those sectors.

May 19. Rockefeller's Commission on Intelligence has do-
cumented CIA/Mafia cooperation in assassination plots.

May 20. Ford vetoes strip mining legislation for the second time.

The House postpones indefinitely action on higher gasoline
taxes and energy conservation, an action that invites the
president to impose import fees.

May 21. Iranian terrorists assassinate two U.S. military
attache's

In the face of administration "reassessment", seventy-
five Senators urge increased aid for Israel.

May 22. The United States accepts a Laotian demand to
negotiate an end to our aid program in that nation.

May 23. Ford questions Portugal's continued presence in
NATO; "I don't see how you can have a Communist element
significant in an organization that was put together for the
purpose of meeting a challenge by Communist elements. . ."

May 24. Ford approves the $405,000,000 Vietnamese re-
fugee aid measure; over 140,000 ultimately are resettled
here.

May 27. Attacking congressional inaction on energy policy,
Ford announces imposition of another dollar import fee and
the phasing out of domestic oil controls beginning in July.
In Paris, Kissinger accepts the idea of "interdependence"
and will consider cooperative efforts to stabilize raw material export prices.

May 28. Agriculture Secretary Butz says that grain export
scandals exist not only in New Orleans but also in every
American port.

May 29. Ford vetoes the $5.3 billion jobs bill as "not an
effective response to the unemployment problem" - - all
economic indicators for the month of May show a slow recovery has begun.

New York State advances $200,000,000 to New York City and
enables it to avert default.

June 1. In Europe since May 28 for a NATO conference,
Ford meets with President Sadat of Egypt and praises his
"sincere desire for peace." Egypt makes clear its willingness to negotiate a Sinai agreement with Israel and reopens
the Suez Canal on June 5.

June 3. The President meets with President Gianni Leone
of Italy and has an audience with Pope Paul VI.

June 4. Ford wins two major congressional victories: the
House sustains his Jobs Bill veto while the Senate fails to
slash the arms procurement budget.

June 6. The Rockefeller Commission releases a 299 page
report on the CIA which documents domestic intelligence gathering, mail openings, burglaries and wiretaps, LSD expe-
riments but not assassination plots. The report says the
Justice Department for twenty years "abdicated its statuary

duties."

Great Britain votes to remain in the Common Market.

June 7. The United States completes the "arms deal of the century" as Belgium, Norway, Denmark and Holland agree to purchase the F-16 from General Dynamics -- the order is potentially worth $20 billion.

June 8. Attorney General Levi asserts that not even the president may authorize an assassination.

June 9-10. The New York Municipal Assistance Corporation, "Big Mac", is created to help the city avoid default.

June 10. The House fails, by three votes, to override the strip mine veto and gives Ford an impressive legislative victory.

June 11. Stanley Hathaway is confirmed by the Senate and takes the oath as secretary of the interior on June 13.

June 12. In the wake of a Supreme Court decision invalidating her election, India's Prime Minister Indira Ghandi, asserts she will remain in office.

Representative L. Nedzi resigns as chairman of the House Select Committee on Intelligence in the wake of the revelations he knew of CIA misconduct. He is ultimately replaced by Representative Otis Pike.

June 13. Ford signs a Veterans/Social Security measure that includes $884,000,000 to maintain the food stamp program.

June 14. At Fort Benning, Georgia, the president extols the volunteer army as "an army of winners."

June 17. Ford tells the National Federation of Independent Businessmen he will not permit the government to become "an instrument of philanthropic collectivism" or "the big daddy of all citizens."

The Mariana Islands vote to accept commonwealth status under the United States.

June 18. Howard "Bo" Callaway, Secretary of the Army, will resign to head the Ford election campaign.

June 19. Ford urges Congress to enact mandatory minimum sentences for violent crimes; he reiterates opposition to firearm registration laws.

June 20. Sam Giancana, a reputed Mafia leader tied to CIA assassination plots, is murdered.

Dixy Lee Ray, State Department Science Advisor since January, quits to protest not being consulted on America's science and energy policies.

June 21. Three Angolan liberation groups sign a cooperative agreement as they prepare for independence from Portugal, due in November.

June 23. Kissinger answers a Turkish threat to close U.S. bases if military aid is not forthcoming: "No ally can pressure us by a threat of termination; we will not accept that its security is more important to us than it is to itself."

The Federal Courts impose limitations on the executive's use of warrantless wiretaps -- Ford, on July 1, orders Justice Department compliance.

June 24. Mozambique becomes independent of Portuguese rule after 470 years.

India's Supreme Court decides that Mrs. Ghandi may remain prime minister, but not vote in Parliament.

June 25. Ford wins his fourth consecutive veto fight with Congress as the House fails to override his negation of the $1.2 billion Emergency Housing Act. Clearly inflationary by Ford's definition, the bill would have created 450,000 jobs and provided mortgage subsidies. The president orders release of $2 billion to finance new mortgages and willingly signs a less inflationary bill on July 2.

June 26. Congress extends unemployment compensation to sixty-five weeks -- a measure that Ford signs.

F. David Matthews is nominated secretary of H.E.W. -- the Senate accepts him and he assumes office on August 8.

Two F.B.I. agents are shot and killed on the Wounded Knee
Indian Reservation. Their alleged assassins are found
innocent in July, 1976.

Mrs. Ghandi proclaims a state of national emergency that
allows her to jail opponents and censor the press. India's
neo-dictatorship lasts until January, 1977, when politicians
are freed and new elections called.

Ford proposes a nuclear fuel bill that will provide "energy
independence." Hearings demonstrate that monetary risks
belong to the government while profits will go to private
individuals and the project dies stillborn.

June 27. The president asks amendment of the Clean Air
Act (1970) to give auto makers five more years to meet
emission standards. The Federal E.P.A. discovers a "massive failure" of present cars to meet standards (July 3).

June 28. Studies recommend separation of Secretary of
State/National Security Advisor posts once Henry Kissinger retires.

June 30. In a controversial snub designed to foster detente,
the White House announces that the president is too busy to
meet with Russian dissident and Nobel Prize winner Alexander Solzhenitsyn.

June industrial prices reverse an eight month decline and
rise 0.4 per cent while unemployment drops to 8.6 per cent
-- the recession is clearly ended.

July 1. Defense Secretary Schlesinger asserts that the
United States, if faced with the loss of a conventional war,
will not renounce its option to first use nuclear weapons.

July 3-4. Ford preaches minimum government which must
"help -- not interfere with -- the lives, the businesses, the
occupations, the professions and the family life of the American people." Our bicentennial year should enhance human
freedom and individual creativity.

July 5. American Mayors meet in Boston and ask a new
federal committment to cities -- "the seeds of New York
are in every American city."

After secret meetings with Israeli leaders, Kissinger calls for territorial concessions on Sinai passes and occupied oil fields. The proposal leads to attacks on our Tel Aviv embassy.

July 6. Rejecting both defense and budget office recommendations, Ford proposes a $1.2 billion nuclear powered cruiser; the question ignored is the wisdom of such great expenditures on one ship.

July 8. The president announces he will run for a presidential term of his own in 1976. Six Democrats have already announced their candidacies while no Republican challenger has emerged.

July 9. "Bo" Callaway declares the president will not seek delegates for Rockefeller.

Ford accepts a congressional compromise that partially lifts the Turkish arms embargo.

July 10. Federal regulatory agencies are ordered not to intrude on the private marketplace except when "well defined social objectives can be attained."

July 11. Congress is angered by administration plans to sell a $350,000,000 air defense system to Jordan and the proposal is tabled on July 28.

July 12. Colonel Ernest Morgan, imprisoned for two weeks by leftist Lebanese in the midst of a continuing civil war, is released.

The Exxon Corp. is accused of giving $45,000,000 in illegal payoffs to Italian politicians from 1963-72.

July 14. Ford proposes total decontrol of domestic oil prices over a thirty month period, but Democrats agree "there is no chance of his selling decontrol."

FBI Director Kelley concedes agency burglaries for "security" purposes.

July 16. The sale of 3,200,000 metric tons of grain to Russia is announced by the Cook and Cargill Companies. Their executives are under investigation for grain export frauds.

The Stock Market hits its 1975 peak.

July 17.   Russian and American astronauts link up in space, a historic interstellar "first. "

July 18.   Senator Church asserts there is no evidence that any president knew of CIA assassination plots.

Helsinki is selected as the site for a thirty-five nation European security conference.

July 20.   In Angola, the truce between factions breaks down and heavy fighting resumes. Unknown then, the "40" Committee, led by Kissinger, has approved on July 17 a $300, 000, 000 grant to our supporters there.

July 21.   Thirteen Bunge Corp. executives are indicted for conspiracy to short-weight grain shipments and hide evidence of the thefts.

The president apologizes to the family of Frank Olson, who died in CIA-sponsored LSD tests.

July 24.   CIA Director Colby says he told the Justice Department of possible perjury by his predecessor in testimony on Chile. Only the previous day, Nixon's directive to the CIA to halt the election of Salvador Allende as Chile's president had been revealed.

The House deals a stunning blow to Ford when it refuses to lift the Turkish arms embargo, by a vote of 223-206.

The Federal Council on the Aging charges the administration with an "apparent lack of consideration for the economic plight of the elderly;" the president rejects the assertion as unconfirmed by data or analysis.

July 25.   Ford vetoes as inflationary a $7.9 billion Education Act.

Calling restrictions on U.S. "unavoidable, " Turkey threatens closure of twenty bases.

Secretary Hathaway resigns after only six weeks in the cabinet. Questions persist as to whether the cause was illness or his refusal to accept patronage appointments.

July 26.   Ford vetoes the Health Bill and the Senate, by a
vote of 67-15, immediately overrides.

The president leaves for a ten day European tour including
visits to West Germany, Poland, Rumania and Yugoslavia.

July 29.   House repassage of the Health Bill completes the
overriding of Ford's thirty-sixth veto -- the first to be
overcome in 1975.

July 30.   Ford's approval rating has risen to 52 per cent
in the wake of his foreign travels, economic upturn and the
Mayaguez.   Problems persist, however, in the continuing
deadlock over oil, the insolvency of New York City, and the
slow pace of economic recovery.

August 1.   Ford, attending the Conference on Security and
Cooperation, signs the vague Helsinki Charter; he asks
that leaders be judged "not by the promises we make, but
by the promises we keep."   When Russia later ignores the
Helsinki human rights "basket," Ford's acceptance is considered a mistake.

August 3.   Agriculture Secretary Butz asks grain dealers
to halt exports to Russia, and George Meany orders a long-
shoreman's boycott of grain loading.

August 4.   In Belgrade, Ford attacks New York City: "They
don't know how to handle money, all they know how is to
spend it."

August 5.   Ford rectifies a "110 year oversight" and restores Robert E. Lee to full citizenship.

August 6.   The president approves a seven year extension
of the Voting Rights Act, a measure which broadens coverage especially for Mexican Americans, Asians and Indians.
He also concludes two days of talks with Japanese Prime
Minister Takeo Miki as he attempts to restore our relationship there after the "Nixon shocks."

August 7.   Ford praises Vice President Rockefeller.   He
denies as a "tempest in a tea pot" all speculation that he
will drop Rockefeller from the ticket to appease the Republican right.

August 8. Ford is variously criticized by the N.E.A., the Urban Coalition, the National Council of Senior Citizens and the National Association of Home Builders as well as by Senator William Proxmire.

August 9. On his first anniversary in office Ford calls himself a "middle of the road conservative" and promises to further reduce "stagflation" in the economy. He defends his thirty-six vetoes as indicative of a "no new program" approach to government.

August 11. The Court of Appeals invalidates Ford's $2.00 surcharge on imported crude oil.

August 15. The president addresses the Vail (Colorado) Symposium and affirms his intention to decontrol domestic "old oil" prices. He accuses Americans of "squandering" energy and attacks congressional delays in enacting an energy program.

Secretary Schlesinger orders the Navy to drop plans for a fleet of super carriers.

August 17. Ford tells Kissinger to resume his "shuttle" diplomacy in the Mideast.

August 18. In a speech to 20,000 farmers in Des Moines, Ford pledges to clean up the grain scandal and terms grain sales a "vital part" of America's diplomacy with the Soviet Union. The AFL-CIO maritime unions begin to boycott grain loadings for Russia.

August 19. Moscow rejects a Kissinger caution to stay out of Portugal's revolution and proclaims "mass solidarity" with Lisbon's Communists. Ford tells the American Legion that Portugal may be a test of the Helsinki accords.

The president jokes ruefully that his wife's TV interview, in which she condoned pre-marital affairs, could cost him twenty million votes.

August 20. An injunction orders the dock workers to load ships with Soviet wheat purchased before July 1.

August 21. Three weeks after the U.S. joined the O.A.S. in lifting economic and political sanctions against Cuba,

the Ford administration lifts restrictions on Cuban trade
by "third countries" or American owned companies abroad.
Despite these overtures, relations with Cuba will not improve under Ford.

August 22. The Vail White House rejects as "vague" a
Rockefeller sponsored plan to achieve energy independence
through a $100 billion Energy Resources Finance Corp-
oration.

August 25. Ford promises hardware dealers in Chicago
to "get the Federal government out of your business, out
of your lives, out of your pockets and out of your hair."
He pledges reduced government, rigorous enforcement of
anti-trust laws and that his "never will be an administration of special interests."

August 26. Responding to Civil Rights Commission cri-
ticism, the White House explains that the president "does
not believe forced busing to accomplish racial balance is
the best way to achieve quality education." This represents a firm position that Ford upholds all during 1976's
presidential campaign.

August 28. Kissinger's "shuttle" succeeds. President
Sadat initials a Sinai accord "with no hesitation at all,"
even though it isolates Egypt among the Arab states.
Israeli agreement is announced September 1.

August 29. Ford ignores recommendations and asks Congress to grant only a 5 per cent pay raise for federal employees.

August 30. William Simon denies the administration has
been "apathetic" toward New York City's financial troubles;
he concedes a default could adversely affect the national
money market.

August 31. Oil price controls expire as the president and
Congress continue their search for agreement on gradual-
ly decontrolled prices. Five major labor leaders denounce
Ford's economic policies as "Herbert Hoover revisited."

September 1. UN Ambassador Moynihan proposes an international agency to spur energy development.

September 2. Ford and Simon tell the IMF and the World Bank that they will not overstimulate American economic recovery in order to advance the world's economy.

September 3. The Republican Wednesday Club warns Ford that a too conservative course can cost him industrial states in 1976; he is asked to keep Rockefeller and to prevent harassment of the vice president by Howard Calloway.

September 4. The Church Committee on Intelligence is granted permission to examine Nixon's presidential papers.

After both Ford and Simon have reiterated their opposition to New York City aid, Congressman Henry Reuss and Speaker Albert demand federal action to prevent a "chain of municipal crises."

Secretary Butz says there will be no further grain shipped to Russia until accomodation is reached with labor. However, on September 5, a federal judge orders ninety more days days of loading in New Orleans.

September 5. On the grounds of the state capitol in Sacramento, Lynette Alice Fromm pulls a gun only two feet from the president. The "assassination" fails and only two hours later the president delivers a prepared address lamenting the growing crime rate.

One day after the Sinai withdrawal package is signed in Geneva, Senator Harrison Williams questions how Ford "can pull Cairo out and let New York down?"

September 6. The National Guard is mobilized to deal with violence that erupts in Louisville after court-ordered busing plans are implemented.

September 8. The Justice Department asks U.S. District Court to reject Richard Nixon's suit for his presidential papers; he "would not be a trustworthy custodian" and has a "propensity to distort the historical record."

Republicans choose Kansas City as the site for their 1976 convention.

September 9. The House overrides Ford's Education Act

veto of July 29, even as the president vetoes a six-month extension of domestic oil price controls.

Ford pledges to obtain long term grain shipping agreements with Russia and extends the moratorium on new sales into October. Meany agrees to halt labor's boycott of already purchased wheat consignments.

September 10. The Senate completes the override of the Education Act veto -- the sixth such veto overturned in thirteen months. However, the Senate fails to overturn the oil control veto, and Ford terms it a "victory for all Americans who depend on energy for their jobs. "

September 11. Wearing a protective vest and ringed by security men, Ford stumps New Hampshire for Senatorial candidate Louis Wyman. He vows, "I'll be back, " an obvious reference to the nation's first presidential primary.

September 12. After the House Select Committee on Intelligence publishes four words not cleared by the intelligence community, the president orders that all classified materials be refused the Committee and orders all administration officials not to testify before it on classified matters. The House immediately subpoenas documents it wants and draws an issue between "national security" and Congress's "right to know. "

September 13. The president tells the National Federation of Women he will use the veto "again and again and again" against Democratic spending; he also attacks "forced busing. " Ford maintains an extraordinary schedule of appearances and there is continuing discussion as to whether the Republican party, taxpayers or his election committee should finance the trips. Since becoming president, he has travelled over 120, 000 miles and spent the equivalent of two full weeks in airplanes.

September 16. John Durkin wins New Hampshire's Senate seat in an election many interpret as a repudiation of Ford.

OPEC is warned against a further rise in crude oil prices.

September 17. Ford's confrontation with the House continues as the Pike Committee turns down his offer of screened documents; the president is technically "not in compliance" with

House subpoenas.

September 18. The FBI captures kidnapped heiress Patricia Hearst, now an accused bankrobber and avowed "radical feminist."

Jordan rejects a U.S. offer of fourteen Hawk missile batteries; limitations on their use were "insulting to national dignity," but changes its policy on September 19.

India sharply criticizes Ford for adverse comments -- "a very sad development " -- on their emergency measures and for cancelling his trip to that nation.

Doctor Linus Pauling receives the Medal of Freedom from Ford, an honor twice denied him by Nixon.

September 20. The Gallup Poll finds that only 21 per cent of Americans consider themselves Republicans, the party's weakest showing since the Depression. Ford asserts he would welcome primary competition from Ronald Reagan.

September 21. At Stamford University, Ford denounces a "Big Brother bureaucracy."

September 22. In San Francisco, Sara Jane Moore fires a shot at Ford despite greatly increased security measures.

Secretary of Commerce Morton refuses to provide Congress with the names of corporations which were asked to participate in the Arab-sponsored boycott of Israel.

September 23. Despite two assassination attempts, Ford asserts he will not be a "hostage" in the White House.

Senator Buckley (R.- NY) endorses Ford's "hands off" policy toward the City.

September 24. It is revealed that the CIA routinely opened foreign correspondence to Americans over a twenty year period, ending in 1973. The Church Committee reveals that the FBI committed at least 238 unauthorized break-ins from 1942-68.

September 25. The president and Congress compromise and agree to restore oil price controls through November 15.

The House reduces the defense budget by $9 billion.

Otis Pike says he will ask the House for contempt citations
if the executive does not release documents to the Committee on Intelligence.

September 26. Phillips Petroleum announces it made illegal
$1,000 contributions to Ford's reelection campaign in 1970
and 1972; the president "had no idea" the funds were tainted.

Daniel Boorstin is confirmed twelfth librarian of Congress
after a bitter two-month fight.

September 27. After a contentious four day conference,
OPEC raises oil prices 10 per cent, an action Ford "strongly regrets." The president denounces congressional refusal to accept the administration's energy policies, but signs
(September 29) the interim price control bill.

September 28. Pike claims the CIA could not warn America
against a sneak attack due to its ineffective bureaucracy,
"above the gathering line."

September 30. The CIA delivers all but fifty words of subpoened documents to Pike's Intelligence Committee and thus
avoids probable censure by the House.

The United States prevents the admission of Vietnam to the
United Nations.

The Senate Foreign Relations Committee asks a Ford pledge
that no secret pacts with either Egypt or Israel are being
withheld from Congress. They wish executive assurance before they vote to approve a pact that will station 200 American monitors between the opposing forces.

The Executive Committee of the AFL-CIO deplores the
"most dangerous [economic] mess in forty years." But
September's industrial production rises for the fifth consecutive month, while unemployment drops to 8.3 per cent.
Later figures show the GNP increase in the third quarter
of 1975 was 17.5 per cent, the greatest gain in twenty-five
years.

October 1. At a meeting of thirty-three suburban mayors
in Skokie, Ford attacks New York City; he tells them, "your

constituents wouldn't tolerate it if you ran your cities as
badly as New York City has been run." At Omaha, Ford
polls an audience on whether the government should "bail
out" the city and leads the laughter when only one hand is
raised.

October 2. W.T. Grant & Co., the seventeenth largest
U.S. retailer, files for bankruptcy.

Mayor Beame denounces the administration's "myopic view
that a financial crisis in the country's largest city would
have no effect on the rest of the nation."

October 3. Ambassador Moynihan attacks Ugandan dictator
Idi Amin as a "racist murderer." When subjected to attacks
in the Assembly, the ambassador receives full presidential
support for his position.

Ford vetoes the $2.7 billion Child Nutrition Act that had
been trimmed to meet his objections.

Ford wins a major congressional victory as a partial lifting of the Turkish arms embargo becomes law and Turkey
is allowed to purchase $185,000,000 of equipment.

October 4. Stuart Spencer becomes Director of Organization for Ford's election campaign.

West German Chancellor Schmidt warns Ford a New York
City bankruptcy could have a "domino effect" in European
finance.

October 5. The Church Committe charges the CIA tried
to murder Fidel Castro, but it has no evidence that any
president knew of or ordered the attempt. At the same time,
it is revealed that the FBI continued counter-intelligence
operations for thirty months after a supposed halt.

October 6. Ford proposes a permanent tax cut of $28 bil-
lion, contingent on congressional promises to slash the budget equally. Democrats label that formula a "mirage" and
"totally preposterous."

October 7. Congress easily overrides the "school lunch
veto" as many Republicans, including both minority leaders,
desert the president.

Nessen announces that the fiscal year 1977 budget will be
$395 billion.

Although he "disapproves" of his son's earlier use of mari-
juana, Ford praises his honesty in admitting its use to the
press.

October 8. FED Chairman Burns concedes a New York default "could trigger a recession."

Ford asks Congress to establish a National Commission on
Regulatory Reform and eliminate strictures on domestic
airlines to spur competition and reduce fares.

October 9. Congress approves the new Geneva accord including its provision to station 200 American technicians
in the Sinai passes.

October 10. Thomas Kleppe and Roderick Hills win confirmation as Secretary of the Interior and head of the SEC.

New York uses grants from the Labor Department to re-
hire 2000 workers.

The president lifts the grain embargo on sales to Poland.

October 11. Rockefeller breaks with Ford and calls for
swift federal aid to New York if they balance their budget
by 1978.

October 12. Governor Connally asserts that Ford should be
"more imaginative, more agressive and more innovative,"
and hints he may run in 1976.

Kissinger asserts that the SALT II talks are 90 per cent
completed. Failure to agree on the nature of the cruise
missile and backfire bomber prevent SALT success during
the Ford administration.

October 14. The president is involved in a minor car ac-
cident in Hartford, Connecticut while campaigning for his
tax program. Once again security arrangements are over-
hauled.

October 17. New York City averts default only an hour before the banks close when teachers retirement pension funds

are made available. Nessen declares New York "a way-
ward daughter hooked on heroin" who "needs to go cold
turkey."

October 19. Watergate Prosecutor Henry Ruth criticizes
as "atrocious" the timing and unconditional nature of the
Nixon pardon.

October 20. The U.S. and Russia announce a five year
grain deal beginning October 1, 1976. Ford lifts his moratorium on grain sales in 1975 and the Soviets immediately
purchase 1,200,000 metric tons. Stocks reach a three month
high at 842.25.

The New York Conservative Party announces it will oppose
Ford's election if Rockefeller is the vice-presidential candidate.

Schlesinger denounces the House for "deep, savage and arbitrary" cuts in the defense budget but the Senate restores
only $406,000,000 of the $7.6 billion cut (October 29).

October 21. The president is ordered to give a videotape
deposition for the trial of Lynette Alice Fromme. He agrees
to this plan on October 28, and gives his testimony on November 1.

Ford's tax and spending reduction plan is termed "hogwash"
by Senator Muskie. There are no fewer than nine announced
Democrats anxious to run against Ford in 1976.

Kissinger, in China to prepare the way for a Ford trip,
meets Mao Tse-tung but little is accomplished due to American detente with the Soviet Union.

October 22. A five year base maintenance agreement with
Spain is submitted to Congress.

October 24. Ford terms "too small" a House-approved
tax cut of $12.7 billion.

Senator Hubert Humphrey says Zaire will get "not one damn
dime" of its $60,000,000 aid unless the administration helps
New York City. Non-candidate Humphrey leads the Democratic field for his party nomination.

October 26. Sadat begins a ten-day tour of America to seek
the economic and military aid implied by the Sinai Agreements. He is feted by Ford but is not officially received
when he visits New York City.

October 27. A Puerto Rican nationalist group, the F.A.L.N.,
sets off nine bombs in three American cities.

The U.S. embassy in Lebanon advises all Americans to
leave that war-torn nation.

October 28. At an unannounced meeting, Rockefeller tells
Ford he will not run in 1976, a decision he was forced into
by unceasing rightwing pressure.

October 29. The National Press Club hears Ford announce,
"I am prepared to veto any bill that has as its purpose a
federal bailout of New York City." Coincidentally, the city
reports its lowest number of employed since record keeping
began in 1950. Beame denounces a "default of presidential
leadership," while Governor Carey calls it "a kick in the
groin" and The Daily News sums it all up: "Ford to City --
Drop Dead."

October 30. Prince Juan Carlos, of Spain, assumes chief
of state power as Francisco Franco nears death.

Ford asks a foreign aid package of $4.7 billion, of which
$3.4 billion will go to the Mideast.

October 31. The Finance Chairman of the Ford election
staff resigns due to conflict with Callaway.

Only a week after its university halted all construction projects, the state of New York suspends for five years all its
housing and rehabilitation projects.

November 2. Secretary Schlesinger and Director Colby
are dismissed in what is soon called the "Halloween Massacre;" Kissinger gives up his post as National Security Advisor. They are replaced by Donald Rumsfeld, George Bush
and Brent Scrowcroft, while Richard Cheney becomes White
House Chief of Staff.

November 3. A presidential press conference confirms the
"massacre" and Ford adds that Elliot Richardson will re-

place Morton as Secretary of Commerce; he now has a team composed of "my guys."

The Church Committee votes to ignore a presidential plan and will deliver its report to the Senate for eventual publication (November 20).

November 4. Busing of 21,200 Detroit students is ordered to begin on January 26.

November 5. Colby agrees to remain at the CIA, pending Bush's confirmation.

Sadat addresses Congress and urges a tempering of support to Israel and more sympathy for the Palestinian cause.

November 6. The Pike Committee denounces "substantial" distortion of Soviet strength and subpoenas Arms Control Agency reports.

Congress approves a Consumer Protection Agency bill, but the bill dies when threatened with a Ford veto.

November 7. Ford announces he will enter all 1976 Republican primaries.

November 9. Appearing on "Meet the Press," Ford claims that if New York defaults, "there will not be any serious ramifications in the money markets." He says his greatest accomplishment has been the "restoration of credibility and confidence in the White House."

November 10. The U.N. General Assembly declares Zionism a form of racism. Ambassador Moynihan says America "does not acknowledge, it will not abide by, it will never acquiese in this infamous act." To Ford, the "resolution undermines the principles on which the U.N. is based."

Portugal leaves Angola and civil war immediately erupts.

November 11. A House subcommittee votes to cite Rogers Morton for contempt after his refusal to deliver documents. Otis Pike also charges that the administration has ignored three of seven subpoenas by his committee.

November 12. William Douglas retires from the Supreme

Court.

The Senate Banking Committee rejects Ford's nominee for
the Home Loan Bank Board on the basis of his attitudes toward public housing and blacks. Three other presidential
nominees are rejected in this time for confrontation.

HEW Secretary Matthews averts a House contempt citation
by delivering subpoened hospital certification documents.

November 13. Ford, calling on Congress to restore free
market competition, proposes reduced regulation of the bus
and trucking industries.

November 14. Action by the New York Legislature averts
defaults by the city of Yonkers and the State Housing Finance Agency. Unless it acts to help New York City, Ford
says, "there is absolutely no change in my position."

Although Republicans criticize the president's professed
willingness to sign compromise oil legislation that will reduce prices, he extends the oil freeze another thirty days
while he studies the legislation.

Pike's Intelligence Committee votes three counts of "con-
tumacious conduct" against Secretary Kissinger for refusing to deliver documents. The State Department condemns the action as "unbelievable."

November 15-17. Ford attends a six nation economic conference at Rambouillet, France, and praises the "penetrat-
ing, friendly and useful" talks. The conference does foster a monetary accommodation with France which calms
the international currency markets.

November 18. The administration refuses to identify nations
that grossly violate human rights yet receive American aid.

November 19. Citing the threat of retaliation, Colby asks
the Church Committee to delete specific names from its
347-page report. He also, "in principle," opposes the publication of the committee's work.

November 20. Ronald Reagan announces his candidacy for
the Republican nomination.

The Federal Election Commission rules that almost all of Ford's 1975 traveling is for "party building" and need not be charged to his 1976 spending ceiling.

November 21. Senator Walter Mondale withdraws as a candidate for the Democratic nomination.

November 22-23. James Schlesinger says his firing was due to controversies over the defense budget and his anger at lack of "political will" that helps the soviet cause.

November 24. Ford meets with Ambassador Moynihan, who has been accused by the British of being a "Wyatt Earp." The president gives Moynihan his "complete confidence" and averts his resignation.

Kissinger warns that the U.S. cannot "remain indifferent" to Russian or Cuban initiatives in Angola.

November 25. The New York Legislature approves a further $2000,000,000 aid package for New York City, which enables Ford to drop his opposition to federal aid. His proposals for short term seasonal loans, totaling $2.3 billion, go to Congress on November 27.

November 26. Lynette Alice Fromme is found guilty of attempted assassination. She is sentenced to life imprisonment on December 17.

Ford says, despite a computer analysis that upholds the Warren Commission, a new probe into both the Kennedy and King murders is acceptable if it can be done "without reopening the whole matter."

November 28. The White House announces that John Paul Stevens will be nominated to the Supreme Court as the "best qualified" successor to Douglas. The Senate agrees and confirms him, by a vote of 98-0, on December 17.

November 29. Ford leaves for a much discussed trip to China; critics ask "what can be accomplished?" On the way, he visits the Alaskan pipeline project, a weapon that will "liberate" America from "unreliable" sources of oil.

November 30. Israel completes its evacuation of the Sinai oil fields. Egypt needs both oil and increased U.S. aid as revenues from the reopened Suez Canal are only a tenth of expected levels.

December 1-3. In China, Ford meets Deputy Prime Minister Teng Hsiao-ping and asserts that his administration will pursue detente with "strength, vigilance and firmness;" he also spends two hours with Chairman Mao Tse-tung. Despite the civilities, no joint communique or further accomodations emerge as a result of the trip.

December 2. Retired Admiral Elmo Zumwalt charges that Kissinger withheld from the president evidence proving Russia's "gross violations" of SALT II. The charge is rejected by both the State Department and James Schlesinger.

Moynihan charges that Russia seeks "to colonize Africa" by sponsoring Cuban intervention in Angola.

December 3. The People's Republic of Laos is proclaimed.

December 4. A $13 billion tax cut bill, without a spending ceiling, is completed. Minority Leader John J. Rhodes predicts that it will be vetoed.

The Church Committee finds no direct CIA involvement in Chile's 1973 coup d'etat.

December 5. As Congress completes a $2.3 billion loan program for New York City, the stock market finishes its worst week since September, 1974. National unemployment remains at 8.3 per cent.

December 7. After stopovers in Jakarta and Manila, Ford visits Pearl Harbor and proclaims a "new Pacific Doctrine." However, Indonesia is invading Timor, our relations with Manila are strained and our position in Asia is non-existent.

The Republican National Committee decides to provide mail-in lists to both Ford and Reagan.

December 8. Moynihan vetoes a Security Council resolution condemning Israel for raids on P. L. O. camps in Lebanon.

Secretary Morton avoids a contempt citation by the House by delivering subpoened documents.

December 9. The New York "bail out" legislation is signed and appropriations are completed by December 18.

December 10. The Pike Committee withdraws pending contempt citations and finds the administration in "substantial
compliance" with its subpoenas.

The Pentagon announces it will sell twenty-five F-15 jets to
Israel.

December 11. Elliot Richardson is confirmed as Secretary
of Commerce, his fourth cabinet post.

Moynihan characterizes the UN General Assembly as "a
theatre of the absurd."

Reagan displaces Ford as first choice among Republican
and Independent voters.

December 12. Legislation abolishing "fair trade" laws in
twenty-one states is signed.

Sara Jane Moore admits in court that she "willfully and
knowingly attempted to murder Gerald R. Ford . . .by
use of a handgun;" she receives a life sentence on January
15, 1976.

The Church Intelligence Committee rejects Nixon's offer
of restricted testimony.

December 13. Howard Callaway accuses Reagan of inept-
ness as California's governor and of being irresponsible;
he also says Reagan would be an acceptable vice president.

December 15. The Senate completes preparation of tax,
energy and picketing legislation.

The FBI admits harassment of actress Jane Fonda for her
anti-war activities.

December 16. Ford decides to accept legislation to reim-
burse New York and seven other cities for the protection
they provide foreign diplomats. However, when the city
presents its claims in December, 1976, they are denied by
Secretary Simon.

December 17. Ford vetoes the tax cut extension bill which
does not include a spending ceiling. The House fails to override and a six month compromise is reached. Congress makes
a non-binding committment to cut spending in line with future

tax reductions. The bill becomes law and the president claims a 100 per cent victory of principle.

December 19. Ford vetoes the $45 billion HEW/Labor appropriation bill.

The Senate breaks a filibuster and cuts off funds for covert operations in Angola. Ford calls the action a "deep tragedy" that will "seriously damage the national interest."

December 22. After a year of negotiations, Ford signs an Energy Policy Conservation Act that rolls back crude oil prices, mandates greater auto appliance efficiency and authorizes a national petroleum reserve.

December 23. Richard Welsh, the CIA station chief in Athens, is murdered shortly after his name was published in a left-wing journal. Ford authorizes burial in Arlington National Cemetery: "...he certainly died in the service of his country."

The first campaign subsidies are paid by the Election Commission; Ford's organization receives $374,000.

December 28. A years end White House publicity campaign seeks to counter Ford's image as "an amiable, vacillating, accident-prone bungler." Press Secretary Nessen defends Ford as "healthy . . . graceful and . . by far the most athletic president within memory." His forty-two vetoes represent not negative government but rather responsible management and effective leadership against a Democratic Congress. He is open and available, a fact proven by twenty-three news conferences and fifty interviews during his sixteen months as president.

December 29. A bomb at New York's LaGuardia Airport kills eleven, injures seventy. Despite all local and federal efforts, no terrorists are found.

December 31. Russia denounces America's failure to complete SALT II.

Ford can count on better economic conditions in 1976. Inflation has been slowed to 7 per cent and America's trade surplus was the largest in history, $11 billion. Stock prices rose 38.3 per cent in 1975, but it was a terrible year for both the automobile and housing industries, a fact mirrored in 8.5 per cent average unemployment.

THE RACE FOR THE WHITE HOUSE

1976   January 2. Ford vetoes a common site picketing bill drafted
              to his specifications. Although the veto pleases conserva-
              tive Republicans, it causes Secretary Dunlop to resign and
              guarantees the antipathy of organized labor to Ford's can-
              didacy.

              January 3. Governors of four large states call for the fed-
              eralization of welfare in America.

              Pravda asks an end to all foreign armed intervention in An-
              gola. Ford says it would be "unwise" to abandon detente
              even though the Angolan experience is "inconsistent" with
              its aims.

              January 5. Ford tells the American Farm Bureau that food
              will not be used as a weapon against Russia. He denounces
              Reagan's proposal for a $90 billion cut in spending as a
              guarantee of more state taxation.

              January 7. Only a day after CIA contributions to anti-Com-
              munist Italian politicians are reported, the Italian cabinet
              resigns -- but over a totally different issue.

              Federal Appeals Court unanimously upholds the constitu-
              tionality of the Presidential Recordings Act of 1974. Re-
              jecting Nixon's suit, the court notes he "might not be a
              wholly reliable custodian" of the materials.

              January 8. Kissinger announces that America will reduce
              foreign aid to nations that fail to support us at the United
              Nations.

              January 9. The stock market reaches its highest point in
              twenty-six months; it has gained 52.42 points in a week.
              As the rally continues, Ford's popularity increases also.

              January 10. Ford meets with the Church Committee and
              they agree to draft legislation reforming America's intel-
              ligence apparatus.

              January 12. America alone votes against seating the P.L.O.
              at the U.N. The Palestinians are granted all membership
              rights except the vote.

Reagan admits his $90 billion proposal was a mistake. It probably costs him the New Hampshire and Florida primaries.

January 13. Ford names Rogers Morton his counselor to deal with energy and with "incidental" political concerns. The Federal Election Commission orders that part of his salary be paid by the Ford Election Committee.

Many of the 1400 delegates at the White House Consumer Conference charge the president with ignorance of consumer concerns.

January 14. Nixon loyalist Anne Armstrong is nominated minister to Great Britain; she wins confirmation January 28.

The SEC reports that at least thirty U.S. corporations are implicated in illegal political contribution schemes and another fifteen have already admitted guilt.

January 15. The Treasury Department opposes Kissinger and says the U.S. must not sign international agreements to set world commodity prices: we must never "sacrifice economic principles for the sake of political gains."

January 16. The stock market completes the busiest week in its history as 159,600,000 shares were traded. Industrial production rose 1 per cent in December as the recession continues to wane.

January 19. Ford's State of the Union address calls for "new realism" about federal spending and a reduction of government programs. "The state of our union is better, in many ways a lot better; but still not good enough."

The P.L.O. and Syria intervene in the Lebanese Civil War. The U.S. engages in "crisis management" to reassure Israel that the limited nature of the action poses no threat to her.

January 20. Governor Jimmy Carter wins the Iowa Democratic caucus, while Ford and Reagan finish virtually even in the Republican straw poll.

The Justice Department decides it will not prosecute CIA

men who plotted foreign assassinations.

January 21. The president requests a budget of $394.2 billion for fiscal 1977, a proposal which includes a deficit of $43 billion and fewer social programs.

January 22. Congress completes a $6.4 billion Railroad Consolidation Act (Conrail).

Kissinger, in Moscow, reports a "considerable degree of progress" toward a SALT II agreement, but this hope is not realized during the bitter election year.

The twenty-fifth Lebanese cease fire goes into effect, but is soon breached.

January 23. The stock market breaks its week old record as 161,680,000 shares are traded. The index has risen over 100 points since January 1.

January 24. The United States signs a five year Treaty of Friendship (military base agreement) with Spain.

January 25. The Pike Committee concludes that intelligence agencies now operate "beyond the scrutiny" of Congress and do not adequately report their budgets. The findings are leaked and featured in the news media.

January 26. The United States vetoes a Security Council resolution favoring an independent Palestinian state.

January 27. Ford is dealt two major defeats as the House overrides his HEW veto and cuts off aid to Angola.

George Bush is confirmed as Director of the CIA. His predecessor, William Colby, was awarded the National Security Medal by a grateful president (January 26).

January 28. The Senate completes the override of Ford's HEW veto. Seventeen Republican Senators and forty-nine representatives defect from the president to help enact the $45 billion appropriation.

January 29. The House delays publication of the Pike Committee Report pending Ford's approval.

The president's Council on Environmental Control recommends a ban on Concorde SST landings in America.

January 30. The Supreme Court upholds the constitutionality of the Campaign Law of 1974 but orders that the Federal Election Commission itself be reconstructed.

Ford vetoes a price support measure on milk. It would
cause "unnecessarily high consumer prices," and is upheld
by the Senate on February 4.

January 31. Unemployment falls to 7.9 per cent this month,
which is also the best month in Stock Exchange history.

February 2. Daniel Patrick Moynihan resigns after a tumul-
tuous eight months as UN ambassador. Ford lauds his
services but suspicions remain that he was too flamboyant
for the State Department.

February 3. Ford uses a CBS news interview to condemn
"abortion on demand" and to argue that limitations on abor-
tions should be left to the "local option" of states.

Kissinger, personally attacked by Pravda on February 1
for his "distorted picture" of Angola, charges that Angola
is the "first time that the United States has failed to respond to Soviet military moves outside the immediate Soviet orbit."

February 4. William Usery becomes secretary of labor.

Transportation Secretary Coleman grants limited landing
privileges to the Concorde SST, a decision that is violent-
ly and successfully protested in New York.

February 5. The House narrowly refuses to deregulate
natural gas, by a vote of 205-201.

The comptroller of the currency testifies that some twenty-
eight national banks are in serious difficulties due to bad
foreign investments, but that the banking system remains
sound.

February 6. Continuing testimony before the Senate Sub-
Committee on Multi-national Corporations ties Lockheed
Aircraft to illegal payments in the Netherlands, Japan,

Italy, Turkey, Mexico and Columbia.

Ford begins a two day compaign swing through New Hampshire and is informed that former President Nixon will visit China just before that primary.

February 7. Contrary to all predictions, it is announced that the new acting premier of China is to be Hua Kuo-feng and not Teng Hsaio-ping.

February 8. Ford says he will not debate Gov. Reagan. He prefers that people examine his presidential record.

February 9. Ford formally submits to Congress his plan for higher social security taxes, extended Medicare benefits and new eligibility guidelines for food stamps.

February 10. Ford signs a defense appropriation of $112.3 billion, which bans further aid to Angola. He charges that Congress "lost their guts;" the cut is a "serious mistake and I think they will live to regret it."

February 11. The Organization of African Unity recognizes the Soviet-backed M.P.L.A. faction as the government of Angola.

Although relief is enroute to the victims of Guatemala's earthquake, which killed over 23,000 on February 4, Ford orders the director of A.I.D. to fly there to assess further needs.

The Village Voice, in New York City, publishes a twenty-one page excerpt from the Pike Intelligence report, materials made available to it by CBS Correspondent Daniel Schorr. The publication is denounced by Kissinger and Ford orders an FBI investigation.

February 12. Ford bares his personal finances to the voters; his net worth is $323,489.

February 13. The president vetoes a $6.2 billion job bill as "an election year pork barrel."

The chairman and vice chairman of Lockheed are forced to resign in the wake of the payoff scandal.

February 14. Ford tells a Florida compaign crowd that
society must "act in its own self-defense" and that the
death penalty for certain crimes is justified.

February 15. Chief Justice Burger denounces congressional inaction on court reform, new judgeships and raising
judicial salaries.

February 17. A complete reorganization of U.S. intelligence is announced by the president; Ford will name a three-
man oversight panel to monitor operations for the executive branch and the "40" Committee will be reorganized.

The administration breaks off negotiations for resumption
of economic aid to India.

February 18. The Federal Environmental Protection Agency
bans pesticides containing mercury.

February 19. The House overrides Ford's Jobs Bill veto
but the Senate fails to do so by three votes.

The House orders its Ethics Committee to investigate the
leak of the Pike Intelligence Report.

February 20. Reagan scoffs at charges that he is "too far
to the right" to be elected; he embarrasses the president
by revealing he twice declined to serve in Ford's cabinet.

The stock market has its sixth record day of trading in
1976 and reaches its highest levels in three years. The
15.8 per cent gain since January is the most dramatic in
exchange history.

February 21. Nixon lands in China and is greeted by Premier Hua.

Kissinger, on a six-nation tour of Latin America, declares
Brazil to be an energing world power and promises semi-
annual consultations with its leaders.

February 22. The disengagement of forces in the Sinai
is completed, and the American technicians are firmly
in place in the Mitla Pass.

February 23. CBS relieves Daniel Schorr of all his news

duties pending the result of the House's investigation of intelligence leaks.

February 24. Ford (55,156 or 49.4 per cent) edges Reagan (53,569 or 47 per cent)in the New Hampshire primary but wins seventeen of twenty-one delegates. Jimmy Carter easily wins the Democratic race.

February 25. William Scranton is formally nominated to the post of U.N. ambassador; confirmation is voted March 3.

After Ford invokes executive privilege to prevent records of intelligence telephone intercepts from going to the House, five government officials refuse to testify on bugging operations.

February 26. Ford publicly criticizes Nixon's China trip as "probably . . . harmful" to his campaign. Senator Barry Goldwater is more harsh: "if he wants to do this country a favor he might stay over there."

The USDA publishes a plan to eliminate 5,000,000 people from the food stamp program and save $1.2 billion.

February 27. The Supreme Court grants Congress an additional three weeks to reconstitute the Election Commission. The extension guarantees continued federal monies to presidential candidates.

Eight former GOP chairmen endorse Ford.

February 28-29. In Miami, Ford calls Fidel Castro "an international outlaw" and "solemnly warns" Cuba against military intervention in this hemisphere.

February figures show inflation drops another 0.5 per cent.

March 1. Ford bows to Reaganite pressure and although it deeply embarrasses Kissinger, declares, "I don't use the word detente anymore."

The president proposes that Congress merge twenty-four educational aid programs into a single block grant. Administrative costs and red tape will be eliminated and more local control achieved.

March 2.   Ford defeats Reagan in both the Vermont (84 per cent) and Massachusetts (62 per cent) primary tests.' Reagan's campaign now openly attacks the "failures" of both Ford and Kissinger in domestic and foreign affairs. Kissinger admits, without Ford's knowledge, that he asked Nixon to prepare a written report on his China trip.

Mozambique shuts its 800 mile border with Rhodesia. There is growing fear of race war in southern Africa.

March 5.   The British pound falls below two dollars for the first time in history.

March 6.   Reagan claims that China honored Nixon as "president in retirement" only to show their dismay at Ford's weak policies toward Russia.

March 7.   Executives of four American oil companies meet with Arab officials in Florida.   By March 12, they negotiate the complete takeover of the Aramco Co. and its oil producing operations by Saudi Arabia.

March 8.   Postmaster General Bailar says the postal service must conform to economic realities and reduce services.

Jewish leaders warn Ford of their opposition to sales of military equipment, particularly six C-130's, to Egypt but the president goes ahead with the sale (March 17).

March 9.   In Florida, Ford wins 53 per cent of the vote in a "come from behind" victory.   At this point, due in part to his full use of presidential patronage, Ford has secured ninety-six delegates to Reagan's forty-one and his nomination seems certain.   Carter defeats George Wallace in a startling Democratic upset.

March 10.   Sworn testimony by Nixon accuses Kissinger of supplying the FBI with names to be illegally wiretapped. Kissinger says Nixon "directed the surveillance of the persons then suggested by Director Hoover." This civil lawsuit will ultimately clear Kissinger and find Nixon guilty.

March 11.   The Dow-Jones Stock index crosses 1000 points for the first time since January 26, 1973, the first of a dozen such trips in 1976.

The Port Authority of New York bans landings by Concorde SST jets.

March 12.   A second explosion in three days at the Black Mountain Mine in Kentucky raises the death toll there to twenty-six -- the mine is sealed.

The Japanese agree to keep secret all U.S. data on the Lockheed scandal pending completion of investigations.

March 13.   Campaign Manager Callaway is accused of using government influence to obtain preferential treatment for his ski resort.   Ford asks him to step down pending the inquiry and replaces him with Stuart Spencer.

March 14.   Egypt breaks its Treaty of Friendship with Russia as it moves towards cooperation with the U.S. Sadat cancels a naval agreement with the Soviet Union on April 4.

France removes the franc from the European currency float.

March 16.   Ford, with 59 per cent of Illinois' vote, decisively defeats Reagan for the fifth consecutive time.   Carter defeats Wallace on the Democratic side.

Harold Wilson resigns as Britain's prime minister.

March 17.   Rockwell International admits illegally entertaining Pentagon military procurement officials.   This parallels similar admissions by the Northrop Corporation.

March 18.   Italy imposes harsh austerity measures after the lira drops 25 per cent in two months.

Frank Church enters the Democratic presidential race.

March 19.   Negotiations between the Rhodesian government and black nationalist leaders break down; both sides ask British mediation.

March 20.   Majority Leader "Tip" O'Neill accuses Ford of blocking campaign finance reform since his successes obviate his need for federal funds.

Thailand orders the United States to end its military presence there and the last American bases close on June 20.

March 22. Mayor Beame of New York announces the city may withdraw from the social security system on March 31, 1978. The Supreme Court approves mandated residency requirements for municipal employees.

The Federal Election Commission distributes $1,000,000 to candidates and then becomes inactive as it has not been reconstituted to meet the January 30 Supreme Court requirements.

March 23. Reagan upsets Ford in North Carolina (52 per cent to 46 per cent) and begins a spectacular comeback. From this time until the convention his rhetoric dominates the Republican campaign and puts Ford on the defensive.

The House sets a budget ceiling of $412.8 billion.

March 24. Ford proposes a $135,000,000 national innoculation program against "swine flu."

The Supreme Court decides that blacks who can prove discrimination are entitled to retroactive job seniority.

March 25. The administration concludes four weeks of orchestrated warnings to Cuba by announcing a total review of its military contingency plans. No basic improvement is made in Cuban policy during the Ford years due largely to their Angolan intervention.

In Lebanon, bloody civil war rages across Beirut's once elegant hotel district.

March 27. The first 4.5 mile section of Washington's subway opens, and Ford commits the government to complete an eighty-six station network.

March 28. The FBI admits it burglarized the Socialist Workers Party at least ninety-two times from 1960-1966.

March 29. At the Pentagon, Ford severely criticizes the House budget ceiling and its reduced defense spending.

March 30. Rogers Morton becomes Ford's campaign director.

Congress enacts a 200-mile sea border; Ford approves it on April 13 and it goes into effect March 1, 1977.

March 31. A national TV address by Reagan attacks Ford's economic, foreign and military defense policies and raises vast sums for his continued campaign.

April 1. Conrail, a merged line formed from seven bankrupt railroads, goes into operation.

The Teamsters launch a national trucking strike, but William Usery negotiates partial agreement within two days.

The Justice Department launches investigations of the FBI's Conintelpro abuses and into a reported equipment procurement scandal.

April 4. As yet another Lebanese "truce" disintegrates into chaos, Syrian troops occupy strategic positions.

April 5. James Callahan becomes prime minister of England. Both England and France charge the EPA with setting discriminatory noise levels against their Concorde SST.

April 6. Ford routs Reagan in Wisconsin, 55 per cent to 45 per cent.

The president casts his forty-seventh veto against a $125 million day-care center measure which imposes "burdensome federal restrictions." He also dedicates the LBJ Memorial Grove along the Potomac River.

April 7. The administration ignores its own policy and decides not to ease federal regulations over the cable TV industry.

Carter achieves a late-count victory in Wisconsin. His campaign temporarily stalls after he endorses "homogeneous neighborhoods" retaining "ethnic purity."

April 9. The president signs a law easing requirements for municipal bankruptcy.

General Omar Torrijos of Panama demands completion of
a new Canal agreement by 1977. Reagan's belligerence
on the issue forces Ford to adopt a similar hard stance
against renegotiation.

Congress approves Ford's "swine flu" program.

April 10. The administration concedes that the SALT II
talks are deadlocked. The SALT stalemate and the dis-
avowal of detente are seen as Reagan victories.

April 12. Ford vetoes an easing of the Hatch Act regulations, which prohibit government employees from active
participation in politics. The House upholds his action
on April 29.

Syrian troops advance over six miles into Lebanon.

April 13. The Senate sets the stage for a new confrontation with Ford as it passes a jobs measure similar to the
one it failed to override in February. However, the House
does not act until June 23.

Ford predicts his Democratic opponent will be Hubert
Humphrey.

Senator Kennedy wins his suit against Ford's "pocket"
vetoes of congressional actions.

April 14. Thomas Gates becomes our first titular ambassador to the People's Republic of China.

April 15. The U.S. concludes agreement in principle for
use of Greek bases in return for aid. The agreement
parallels one concluded with Turkey on March 26, but both
are ultimately tabled by Congress.

April 16. The American embassy in Moscow protests, for
the sixth time in three weeks, harassment of its staff by
Russian officials.

New York City successfully repays $275,000,000 in federal
loans as it begins the slow road to financial recovery.

April 18. Pravda accuses America of violating the spirit
of the Helsinki agreements by incessantly warning western

European nations against Communist participation in their governments.

April 19. The Commerce Department reports a GNP gain of 7.5 per cent in the first quarter of 1976 while inflation is held to an average of 3.7 per cent. On the basis of this good economic news, the Dow Jones Index breaks 1000 the next day.

April 20. The Supreme Court unanimously upholds the federal government's right to construct minority housing in white suburbs.

A national strike of rubber workers begins; it soon affects forty- seven plants in twenty-one states.

Ford received a return of $11,600 on his 1975 federal income tax of $94,000. The White House suggests that Reagan should release his tax records.

April 22. The Senate Intelligence Committee reveals existence of an FBI network of journalist/informers that operated through 1973.

April 23. Kissinger leaves for a trip to Africa; his departure signals new American awareness of that continent's economic and strategic importance. The secretary openly commits America to the achievement of black majority rule in Rhodesia.

April 24. Reagan wins twenty- seven of Arizona's twenty-nine delegates to the Republican Convention. He adds delegate strength in Oklahoma, South Carolina and Missouri as well.

President Franjieh of Lebanon signs a constitutional amendment that grants to Parliament the right to select a new president.

April 25. Portugal, once thought certain to go Communist, holds its first free election in fifty years and votes into office a Socialist coalition.

April 26. The Church Committee issues its report on 900 covert operations by American intelligence agencies in the last fifteen years. It attacks both executive and legislative laxity and demands new oversight laws.

April 27. Ford is "disturbed" by proposals of an 8 per
cent rise in steel prices; his reaction reduces the rise to
6 per cent.

The president leaves for four full days of stumping in
Texas, knowing that he will win the Pennsylvania delegation
virtually conceded him by Reagan. Carter's victory in the
Keystone State is his first in a northern industrial state.

April 28. Congress approves a $4.4 billion foreign aid
package.

April 30. The Supreme Court refuses for the second time
to release Federal Election Commission funds until the
commission is reconstituted.

The United States offers to normalize relations with Angola
if Cuban troops are withdrawn.

May 1. Contrary to all predicitions and despite Ford's
harsh personal attacks, Reagan sweeps all ninety-six delegates in the Texas primary.

Interior Secretary Kleppe concedes his funding of Georgia
land purchases is intended to help Ford in the upcoming
primary.

May 2. Despite Naval claims to the contrary, Pentagon
figures show it has constructed more and larger ships than
the Soviet Union since 1969. Despite this and GAO evidence of poor management and cost overruns, the administration, on May 4, requests an additional $1.2 billion for
naval construction.

May 4. Reagan defeats Ford in Georgia, Alabama and
Indiana and wrests the delegate lead from the president.

Congress sends Ford an Election Commission Bill that
will provide subsidy payments to all candidates which
clearly will help Reagan. The president delays signing
it for a week.

The House overrides Ford's day care veto, 301-101, but
the Senate upholds it, 60-34 (May 5).

May 6. Congress agrees on a budget ot $413.3 billion for fiscal 1977, a level far beyond Ford's proposals and sure to prolong their veto battle.

An earthquake in northern Italy claims over 1000 lives.

May 7. Ford casts his forty-ninth veto against the foreign aid bill because of its "unprecedented restrictions" on presidential freedom in policy making.

May 8. Ford charges that Reagan would be "a babe in the woods" in dealing with Congress and likens himself to Truman in 1948. His campaign now emphasizes the themes of "peace, prosperity and trust."

FBI Director Kelley apologizes to America for Hoover's "clearly wrong and quite indefensible" abuses of power. He later concedes the apology was made to forestall hostile legislation by Congress (June 16).

Lebanon, amid gunfire and death, elects Elias Sarkis as president; he is seen as Syria's puppet.

May 10. The Lockheed scandal results in the indictment of Yoshio Kadama in Japan, but a Dutch investigation clears Prince Bernhardt (husband of the Queen) of complicity.

May 11. Reagan, without the help of Democratic crossovers, wins Nebraska's primary but Ford breaks his string of defeats with a triumph in West Virginia.

An Office of Science and Technology is recreated in the White House. Ford, on August 5, appoints Dr. Grayford Stever its director.

May 12. Ford signs the bill creating the Consumer Product Safety Commission.

May 13. The president sends Congress a proposal to reform regulatory agencies. Ford also tells the American Jewish Committee that America "will remain the ultimate guarantor of Israel's freedom."

May 15. Ford becomes the first president since Truman to campaign by train as he crosses southern Michigan, his "must win" state.

May 16. Kissinger, now an embarrassment to Ford's campaign, says he prefers to leave the State Department even if Ford is nominated and elected.

May 17. Ford officially names the members of the reconstituted FEC and so makes possible the resumption of federal subsidies.

The British pound falls below $1.80.

May 18. The president resumes control of the campaign by winning primary victories in Michigan (65 per cent) and Maryland (58 per cent). He has "refloated the Titanic" and predicts a first ballot victory.

The European Economic Committee rejects American pleas to limit their special steel exports.

May 19. The Senate creates an Intelligence Oversight Committee.

May 20. Ford tells Kentucky reporters, "I am totally opposed to court ordered forced busing, " and reminds them he has ordered the attorney general to seek a test case on busing to achieve school integration.

May 21. The newly created FEC distributes monies to candidates. The largest check, for $1,300,000, goes to the Ford campaign.

May 23. The commandant of West Point concedes that a widespread cheating scandal exists at the academy. Before the summer ends almost 200 cadets leave.

Weekend caucuses restore the delegate lead to Ford.

May 24. The Concorde SST begins scheduled flights to Washington.

The uncommitted New York delegation, dominated by Rockefeller, decides to cast 119 votes for Ford.

May 25. On the biggest primary day of the year, Ford and Reagan split six primaries; the drawn results fundamentally favor the Ford candidacy. Reagan's injudicious remarks about TVA probably cost him Tennessee and perhaps

Kentucky. On the Democratic side, Carter amasses an additional 137 delegates and seems certain to be his party's nominee.

Representative Wayne Hayes admits an affair with a staff member which will ultimately drive him from Congress.

May 26. Twenty-six states and three cities sue to halt the imposition of new food stamp restrictions on June 1; a stay is granted.

Ford, campaigning in Ohio, denies that his opposition to forced busing fosters disobedience to law, yet indicates the Justice Department might seek a review of the 1954 Brown decision on segregated schools. This notion is retracted the next day.

May 27. The City University of New York shuts down for two weeks because it cannot meet its payroll. Only the day before, Moody's Investment Service had again downgraded "Big Mac" bonds.

May 28. The United States and Russia sign a five-year treaty limiting the size of underground nuclear blasts. The administration delayed the signing, claiming "technical difficulties", until after the last group of primaries.

OPEC nations agree not to increase prices in 1976 and Ford lauds their "responsible" decision.

May 29. The Justice Department decides not to use Boston as a test case on busing but the president orders "an active search for a busing case suitable for judicial review."

May 30. The seven-month "Cod War," which has caused ruptured relations between Iceland and Britain, ends when the latter withdraws its ships from the North Atlantic.

The U.N. Conference on Trade and Development rejects America's proposal for an international development bank.

May 31. Syrian troops occupy northern Lebanon and establish a cease fire. Syria's intervention has the tacit support of both Israel and the United States.

June 1.   Reagan wins Montana (63 per cent) and South
Dakota (51 per cent) but the president holds Rhode Island
(66 per cent) and increases his delegate strength.

June 2.   The King and Queen of Spain begin their state visit to the U.S.

June 3.   The United States threatens to leave the I.L.O.
if the May 29 decision not to seat the P.L.O. is reversed.
The P.L.O. is seated and we do not leave.

June 5.   The Teton Dam in Idaho bursts. The disaster
causes fourteen deaths, property damage of $1 billion and
is attributed to poor design by the Army Corps of Engineers.
Ford signs a compensation measure on September 9.

June 6.   Despite an ad campaign that portrays Reagan as
willing to risk war over Rhodesia, Ford indicates he is
still considering him for the vice presidency. He defends
parents rights to send their children to segregated academies.

June 7.   The United States leads the "Group of Ten" industrial nations in providing short-term credit of $5.3 bil-
lion so that Britain can support the pound, which has dropped to $1.71.

Ford approves a quota system limiting specialty steel imports from Europe, a political decision that seems to have
little economic justification.

June 8.   Ford wins primaries in New Jersey and Ohio, but
Reagan takes a bloc of 167 California delegates. The thirty
Republican primaries have failed to choose a winner but
the delegate count, 965-862, favors Ford. The president
and Reagan begin to compete for the uncommitted delegates.

Kissinger, addressing the OAS in Santiago, attacks Chilean
violations of human rights.

The head of the Anti-Trust Division resigns in protest of
Ford's equivocal policies of regulation.

June 9.   Secretary Coleman announces he will not decide on
the issue of air bags in automobiles until January, long
after the election.

June 10. An Arab League "peacekeeping" force arrives in Beirut.

June 11. Arthur Burns of the Federal Reserve praises Congress' budgetary restraint and effective control procedures.

Senator Robert Griffin replaces non-delegate John Tower as Ford's floor manager for the Kansas City Convention.

June 12. Reagan wins eighteen of nineteen Missouri delegates after both candidates make personal appearances.

June 13. Representative Allan Howe (D-Utah), is jailed on charges of soliciting the services of a prostitute; the incident costs him his seat in November.

June 14. The Supreme Court refuses to review busing in Boston despite Ford's campaign against "forced" busing orders. Attorney General Levi indicates courts have used busing, according to law, only as a "last resort."

Ford requests Congress to require that corporations disclose any "questionable payments" abroad but does not ask that any sanctions for bribery be enacted. Senator Proxmire labels it "a cop-out."

June 15. The United States assails the I.L.O. for its "unforgivable" bias that ignores forced labor conditions in Communist nations.

Ford tells the Southern Baptist Convention that "we stand in danger of losing the soul of America to the seductions of material gain and moral apathy."

June 16. The American ambassador to Lebanon is murdered.

South Africa begins a series of racial confrontations that will punctuate the summer. In five days of riots in the black township of Soweto, 176 die and 1200 are injured. The use of Afrikaans as a school teaching language is ended.

June 18. Courts rule the USDA "exceeded its congressional mandate" in revising the food stamp program and orders an end to proposed cutbacks.

Ford ignores the Iowa delegate caucus to monitor the Lebanese situation. On June 20, 263 Americans are evacuated.

June 19. After a ten-month trip, Viking I enters Martian orbit.

Ford edges Reagan in Iowa, 19-17, but the latter's gains elsewhere cut the president's total margin to less than seventy votes.

June 20. Victory in West Virginia enables Ford to again halt Reagan's momentum.

June 21. An adult swine flu vaccine is approved.

The Christian Democrats narrowly defeat Communists in elections for the Italian House of Deputies (263-228) and Senate (135-116).

June 23. America casts its fifteenth Security Council veto and prevents Angola's entry into the United Nations.

Carter criticizes the "secretive" and "amoral" diplomacy of Kissinger, the "Lone Ranger" of our foreign policy. The secretary meets with Prime Minister John Vorster of South Africa.

June 24. Ford's legislation to reduce busing and safeguard "domestic tranquility and the future of American education" is sent to Congress. Roy Wilkins of NAACP calls it a "craven, cowardly, despicable retreat and a capitulation to lawlessness, ignorance and the forces of race."

Reagan says there is "no way" he will accept the vice presidency.

June 26. Ford wins a divisive battle in Minnesota but Reagan forces sweep the delegations of Idaho, Montana and New Mexico.

June 27. Ford chairs an economic summit of six western nations. He urges international cooperation against inflation.

Arab militants hijack a plane and fly its 257 passengers to Uganda.

June 28. Pursuant to a law signed by Ford in October, women enter America's service academies.

June 29. America vetoes another Security Council resolution, calling for Israel's immediate withdrawal from Arab territories occupied since 1967.

The GAO criticizes army plans to purchase an untested battle tank.

The Dow Jones passes 1000 for the ninth time this year. All economic indicators except unemployment indicate economic revival.

June 30. Twenty-nine Communist nations, after two days of European talks, endorse "free choice of different roads in the struggle for social change " and continued detente with the United States.

Ford signs a tax measure that extends lower withholding rates.

Senator Barry Goldwater, leader of conservative Republican sentiment, endorses Ford.

July 1. Ford opens the Smithsonian's Museum of Air and Space.

Congress approves a $32.5 billion military appropriation which funds the B-1 bomber and seventeen additional ships. The Senate also approves, by a vote of 57-34, General George Brown as head of the Joint Chiefs of Staff, despite his open criticism of Jewish influence in America. One of Ford's great achievements is his ability to obtain full defense appropriations from Congress.

Secretary Simon renews the federal loan program to New York City.

July 2. The fiftieth Ford veto is cast against a $3.3 billion military construction bill. The Senate sustains the president on July 22.

The Supreme Court, by a vote of 7-2, upholds the constitutionality of the death penalty.

July 3. Israeli paratroopers fly 2300 miles and free hostages held at Entebbe Airport, Uganda.

Ford vetoes the mineral leasing bill despite pressure from western states.

July 4. America's bicentennial celebration includes speeches by Ford in Philadelphia and his review of Operation Sail in New York Harbor.

July 5. Jose Lopez Portillo is elected president of Mexico.

The U.S. Conference of Governors calls for consolidation of the nations welfare system.

A Communist becomes speaker of the Italian Chamber of Deputies.

July 6. Queen Elizabeth II begins a tour of the United States and claims the bicentennial "should be celebrated as much in Britain as in America." She visits Ford on July 7.

Ford vetoes the National Fire Prevention and Control appropriation for its infringement on executive authority. He overrules the Office of Civil Rights and allows father/ son and mother/ daughter events.

The Treasury announces the budget deficit for fiscal 1976 will be $68 billion, a figure later reduced to $65.6 billion.

July 8. The New York Appelate Court allows the disbarment of Richard Nixon.

Ford wins twelve of eighteen North Dakota votes. He retains a lead of about forty delegates.

July 9. Ford orders continuation of the swine flu program despite its insurance problems and the unexpected after-effects of on some people.

The president declares Reagan is qualified to be president, and asks that he keep an open mind about the vice presidency.

July 10. Angola executes four mercenaries, including one American, for participation in its civil war.

July 11. After internecine fighting, Robert Hartmann is divested of his sole authority to issue presidential campaign statements, though he retains control of speechwriting.

July 12. American pressure fails to reverse a decision which bans Taiwan from participation in the Olympics.

Stocks hit a forty-one month high at 1,011.21.

The Security Council debates the Israel raid on Entebbe. Ambassador Scranton lauds the event as "a combination of guts and brains . . . seldom if ever surpassed."

July 12-14. The Democratic Convention in New York City nominates Jimmy Carter for president and adopts a platform which emphasizes employment programs, welfare reform and aid to American cities. Carter, the first nominee from the deep south since 1848, names Walter Mondale his vice presidential running mate.

July 16. Stung by continued revelations of FBI misdeeds, and embarrassed by the fact he was denied full information, Kelley dismisses his associate director. On August 8, he claims he was "deliberately deceived" by his own agents.

July 17. Twenty-four third world nations boycott the opening of the Olympics to protest the participation of New Zealand, whose athletic teams visited South Africa; ultimately twenty-nine nations leave the games.

Ford wins Connecticut's thirty-five delegates while Reagan takes Utah. The final primary results are 1102 for Ford, 1063 for Reagan with ninety-four still uncommited.

July 19. The AFL-CIO endorses Carter for president. Ford is attacked for "the worst recession in 35 years" and "seeking to impose minority rule through an abuse of the veto power."

July 20. Viking I successfully lands on Mars and photographs its surface. Ford proclaims Space Exploration Day.

July 21. The Senate overrides the Public Works veto, by a vote of 310-96, as fifty-seven Republicans desert Ford.

July 22. The Senate overrides Ford's Public Works veto, by a vote of 310-96, as fifty-seven Republicans desert Ford.

Justice Powell delays 116 death sentences in three states pending further court action.

The army unexpectedly delays choosing its new battle-tank in order to consider some European-built components.

July 24. The Gallup Poll reports that 55 per cent of Americans still believe Ford's pardon of Nixon was wrong. Carter claims he will ignore the issue, but Democratic speakers constantly refer to it during the long campaign.

An American Legion Convention concludes its Philadelphia meeting. Its aftermath is a mysterious "Legionnaire's Disease," which ultimately kills twenty-nine participants. Not until January, 1977, do scientists isolate the bacterium that caused the deaths.

July 25. Guards kill an intruder who scales the White House fence.

MIA relatives are told by Ford that he will obtain a full accounting from Vietnam.

July 26. In the continuing aftermath of the Lockheed scandal, former, Japanese Prime Minister Tanaka is arrested.

The Justice Department decides not to prosecute CIA personnel for 250,000 unauthorized mail openings from 1953-73.

Reagan stuns the political world by selecting liberal Senator Richard Schweiker as his running mate if he is nominated.

July 27. Former Texas Governor Connally endorses Ford.

July 28. The chairman of the uncommitted Mississippi delegation endorses Ford.

Vast earthquakes rock China, south of Peking. It is ultimately admitted that over 655,000 people died.

July 29. The House reprimands Robert Sikes (D-Florida), for financial misconduct. Sikes is ousted from his military construction appropriations chairmanship in January, 1977.

July 31. Ford asks 5000 Republicans to send him their vice presidential choices.

Yugoslavia demands recall of the American ambassador for critical remarks.

August 3. The Senate, by a vote of 75-18, overrides Ford's mineral leasing veto.

Secretary Coleman presides over a hearing on the value of air bags in automobiles, and clashes with consumer advocate Ralph Nader

August 4. The House approves the Mineral Leasing Bill -- the tenth override of a Ford veto.

Carter predicts that Ford, "just a quiescent extension of the policies of Nixon, " will receive the Republican nomination.

August 5. After two large atomic tests by Russia, Ford orders an intelligence review to see if the spirit or the letter of the pending underground test treaty has been violated.

August 6. Reunited Vietnam completes its reconciliation with Southeast Asian nations as it establishes diplomatic relations with Thailand.

August 7. One day after the Shah rejected a Senate report critical of arms supplies to Iran, the administration announces a new $10 billion arms deal that will run for six years.

Viking II enters Martian orbit preparatory to its successful landing on September 3.

August 8. Ford addresses 100, 000 Catholic worshipers at a "World Mass" during the Philadelphia Eucharistic Congress. He condemns America's "increased irreverance for life. "

Kissinger acknowledges that the U.S. supplied materials probably were essential to India's atomic program, but he appeals to Pakistan not to construct similar weapons.

Another mobster implicated in CIA assassination plots is found murdered.

August 9. The Ford campaign rejects Reagan's demand that it name a vice president before the convention.

August 10. Senator Buckley will allow his name to be presented for the Republican nomination.

"General abuse" of the cadet honor system is admitted at West Point.

August 11. World problems include new riots in Capetown, battles between Rhodesia and Mozambique, the proposed partition of Lebanon and a Palestinian attack on an El-Al jet. Ford announces he will break tradition and go to the Republican Convention early in order to hold his delegates.

FBI Director Kelley announces a major internal reorganization of the FBI.

August 12. The Firestone rubber workers settle a strike begun on April 21, while coal miners end a four week wildcat strike.

Rumsfeld has a thyroid operation which effectively removes him as a vice presidential candidate.

August 16-17. As the Republican Convention opens, Senator Buckley drops his presidential bid. The president seems certain of the nomination when his forces soundly defeat Reagan's attempt to make him disclose his vice presidential choice before nomination. The platform includes conservative foreign policy positions disliked by Kissinger.

August 18. Ford defeats Reagan on the first ballot by 1187-1070. He meets with Reagan but does not offer him the vice presidency.

Two American officers are murdered in the DMZ dividing Korea.

August 19. Ford selects Kansas Senator Robert Dole as vice president and an unenthusiastic convention endorses his choice. Ford's effective acceptance speech restores confidence and his offer to debate Jimmy Carter is quickly accepted.

August 20. Kissinger demands "explanations and reparations" from North Korea for the incident of August 18. President Kim Il Sung terms the deaths "regretful" and a separation of forces is concluded on September 6.

Southwest Africa (Namibia) rejects "inadequate" South African proposals for its independence.

August 21-22. While resting at Vail, Ford evolves a "presidential" campaign strategy; Dole will attack Carter and appeal to the farm belt while Ford will be temperate and concentrate on the large industrial states.

August 23. Blacks launch a three-day boycott of Johannesburg's industrial plants but Zulu vigilantes attack the strikers and perhaps one hundred persons die.

August 24. The Civil Rights Commission accuses the administration of undermining desegregation by exploiting anti-busing sentiment.

Carter tells a booing American Legion Convention he will pardon Vietnam draft resisters.

August 25. James A. Baker replaces Morton as campaign director.

August 26. Prince Bernhard of the Netherlands resigns his military/business positions after an investigation criticizes his "unacceptable" Lockheed connections.

August 27. Ford criticizes Carter's "flip-flops" which cause public "fear and apprehension" of his candidacy. During the next ten weeks, the president will successfully make Carter the campaign issue.

August 29. Ford travels to Yellowstone Park to announce a plan to double national parkland in a decade. This "bicentennial birthday present" to future Americans reverses his stated opposition to new programs.

August 30. Ford condemns, as "half a loaf," a congressional extension of tax cuts through 1977. He asks a further tax reduction of $28 billion to go along with $28 billion of spending cuts.

The Federal Election Commission rules that the League of Women Voters can sponsor a series of presidential debates.

August 31. Kissinger pledges that America will "bring about peaceful change, equality of opportunity and basic human rights in South Africa. "

FBI Director Kelley is personally accused of improper use
of government services and property.

September 1. Congress approves a tax bill including penalties for American corporations which comply with the
Arab boycott of Israel, a "sunshine" bill which requires
most of fifty federal regulatory boards to conduct their
business in public and a $104.3 billion defense measure
which "goes slow" on the B-1 bomber.

September 2. Dayton's schools peacefully desegregate under a busing order, as did Louisville's earlier.

September 3. August unemployment rises to 7.9 per cent
while prices of industrial commodities rise 0.7 per cent.
Experts are unhappy with the figures and the campaign
will be fought out in a time of economic "pause."

September 4. Ford decides there is "no adequate justification" to remove Kelley as FBI director despite his lapses
of judgment.

September 5. Reports by Congress and the Interior Department indicate that the opening of the Alaska pipeline will
be delayed by the necessity of inspecting for defective welds.

September 6. Carter's formal campaign begins in Warm
Springs, Ga.; his address denounces Ford's timid leadership, "no one seems to be in charge."

September 7. American businessmen support Ford by 66
per cent to only 8 per cent for Carter.

Ford orders that political asylum be granted a Soviet pilot
who defected by flying his MIG-25 to Japan.

A day after Kissinger completed talks with Vorster, five
African presidents call for a diplomatic "shuttle" for
southern Africa. Ford pledges a "major effort" and Kissinger leaves on September 14.

September 9. Mao Tse-tung's death ushers in a period of
turmoil in China.

September 10. R.J. Reynolds Co. admits $25,000,000 in
illegal political payments since 1968.

Ford meets with a delegation of Catholic bishops who are
"encouraged" but "not totally satisfied" by his abortion
position. They had expressed "disappointment" after a
similar meeting with Carter but take an "absolutely neutral"
position on the election.

September 12. Former Watergate Prosecutor Leon Jaworski
says either Nixon or his secretary caused the famous "gap"
on the tapes.

September 13. Ford signs the "sunshine" law and casts his
fifty-sixth veto against government funding for a prototype
electric automobile engine. The president uses the Rose
Garden for bill signings in order to remain constantly before the public.

September 14. Faced by an assured U.S. veto, the Security
Council delays consideration of Vietnam's membership until
after November.

Congress approves another sixty-nine months of revenue
sharing.

September 15. Ford formally opens his presidential campaign with a speech at Michigan University. Pledging himself to "specifics, not smiles," he tells students, "trust
is not having to guess what a candidate means."

Daniel Shorr defies the House Ethics Committee and refuses to divulge the source that delivered to him the Pike
Committee's report.

September 16. Congress sets a budget ceiling of $413.1
billion for fiscal 1977. They complete and send to the president their tax and anti-trust measures. The House, by a
vote of 307-101, easily overrides Ford's veto of the electric
automobile bill.

September 17. Ford asserts that Congress's acceptance of
his $104 billion military budget proves his leadership.
"What is more moral in foreign policy than to have peace
with freedom and security?"

Federal District Court denies a final attempt by minor
party candidates to block the presidential debate scheduled
for September 23.

The Senate completes the override of Ford's electric car
veto and so puts the government into competition with private enterprise.

September 19. Sweden's Social Democratic Party loses its
majority for the first time in forty-four years.

Reagan, although supporting the ticket, announces he is
too busy to campaign in five critical states.

September 20. The Army Vice Chief of Staff asserts that
every "responsible soldier" opposes construction of a hy-
brid battle tank using German built components.

A major campaign issue emerges unexpectedly after a
Carter interview in Playboy magazine; the candidate concedes he looked with "lust" at women and hence commited
adultery in his heart.

September 21. The Dow Jones Index soars to 1014.79, its
highest level since January 23, 1973, but in England the
pound sinks to a record low.

September 22. The House Ethics Committee fails three
times to vote against Shorr and closes its investigation
without uncovering the source of the intelligence leaks.

A coalition of eight groups accuses the administration of
eighty-two "counts" of anti-consumer behavior.

September 23. The first presidential debate in sixteen
years is held in Philadelphia's Walnut Street Theatre. Two
polls show that Ford wins the close but rather dull debate
viewed by some 85,000,000 Americans.

U.S. Steel admits it gave Ford five golfing holidays during
his last ten years in Congress. In addition, Ford is the
subject of two Watergate prosecutor probes into the finances
of his congressional campaigns.

September 24. Heiress Patricia Hearst is sentenced to
seven years for bank robbery.

Rhodesia accepts Kissinger's plan to transfer power to black majority rule within two years.

September 25. The Census Bureau reports that 12.3 per cent of America lives below the federal poverty line, and that 2, 500, 000 citizens fell into poverty in 1975.

September 26. The president campaigns through the South aboard a Mississippi paddle wheeler. He tells crowds that "law abiding citizens . . . should not be deprived of the right to have firearms." Ford opposes all gun registration laws but wants greater penalties against those who use guns to commit crime.

September 28. In Lebanon, Syrian and Christian forces assault P. L. O. positions in a last spasm of the civil war.

Congress fails to halt Ford's plan to sell 650 Maverick missiles to Saudi Arabia.

September 29. Ford vetoes the HEW appropriation of $56 billion for reasons of "fiscal integrity." He does order a 4.83 per cent rise in federal civilian and military pay to keep them at par with the private sector.

September 30. Carter accepts the president's denial of all improprieties in the golfing and campaign finance investigations; subsequent statements by the Watergate prosecutors (October 14) and the FBI confirm Ford's denials.

Congress overrides the HEW veto by 67-15 and 312-93.

October 1. Stockpiling three years supply of ninety-three strategic materials wins Ford's approval.

The president personally rebukes Earl Butz for obscene remarks about blacks, but the small black support for Ford evaporates.

October 2. Ford reluctantly signs a $3.7 billion public works measure.

Congress attacks nine regulatory agencies for "lack of sufficient concern" with the public and too great a care for the interests they were created to control.

October 3. The Social Democratic coalition retains power
in the German elections.

October 4. Butz resigns as Secretary of Agriculture.

The president signs the "positive and long overdue" tax
bill.

The Supreme Court refuses to reconsider its death penalty
decision and virtually guarantees that an American will be
executed sometime before Ford leaves office.

October 5. The Allied Chemical Corp. is fined $13,375,000
for polluting the James River.

The GAO accuses the administration of not exhausting all
diplomatic possibilities before using force to free the
Mayaguez. Kissinger disputes the report as based on "misleading information."

Fallout from China's nuclear tests is detected in the eastern
United States.

October 6. The second debate is held in San Francisco and
a Carter "victory" results. Ford commits the greatest
gaffe of the campaign by saying there "is no Soviet domination of Eastern Europe and never will be under a Ford administration."

Rhodesia asserts that its deal with Kissinger is not negoti-
able, either by the African states or the British mediator
at the Geneva negotiations.

October 7. The Commerce Department ignores Ford's promise to reveal the names of firms who cooperated with the
Arab boycott of Israel. Secretary Richardson intends to
release only the names of future compliers, although seven
names are made available immediately.

October 8. The stock market closes at 952.38, a loss of
fifty-five points in two weeks.

The last unemployment statistics before the election show
7.8 per cent national unemployment and a drop in the absolute number of employed Americans. Despite the "pause"
in economic growth, Carter's lead continues to shrink.

October 9. Ford proclaims restriction of imports to maintain high beef prices.

The head of the Ukrainian Americans announces his personal switch from Ford to Carter.

Hua Kuo-feng becomes party chief as well as prime minister of China. He oversees the purge of the "Shanghai
Radicals, " including Mao's widow.

October 11. Ford announces new arms sales (including
concussion bombs) to Israel, but not the Pershing missiles
they requested.

October 12. The president campaigns in New York City,
where eggs are thrown at him; the city is flooded with re-
productions of The Daily News "Drop Dead" headline.

The Watergate convictions of Ehrlichman, Haldeman and
Mitchell are upheld.

The swine flu innoculation program is halted in nine states
due to unexpected deaths following vaccination.

October 13. In New Jersey, Ford says Carter will raise
taxes so he can "spend, spend, spend" on new giveaway
programs. The president reverses policy and raises price
supports for wheat (50 per cent) and corn (20 per cent)
farmers.

October 14. The president holds his first televised news
conference since February 19, a response to Carter's
charge he "hides" in the White House. Ford cites the clean
bill of health given him by the Watergate prosecutor, and
accuses Carter of "slandering the good name of the United
States" with wild campaign rhetoric.

October 15. Cuba cancels its anti-hijacking pact with the
United States.

The stock market continues to fall and closes at 937.

The vice presidential candidates debate in Houston; Mondale
"defeats" Dole.

Ford orders Clarence Kelley not to deliver a speech critical of the FBI's press coverage.

October 16. Ford rejects a Carter telegram alleging "misleading and erroneous statements;" he asserts Carter "will say anything anywhere to be president."

October 18. Ford decides not to reprimand General George Brown, who, in a just published interview, asserted that the Israeli army was a liability for the United States.

October 19. The United States, France and Britain veto a Security Council resolution which would impose an arms embargo on South Africa.

October 20. Ford holds his second press conference in six days to attack Carter as "naive" in foreign policy. He asserts his Mideastern policies are so successful that chances of another oil embargo "are virtually nil."

The president signs the first major revision of copyright laws in sixty-seven years.

October 21. The president announces administration support for the Westway highway project; its $1.4 billion cost will create many jobs for New York City's faltering economy.

The Gallup Poll finds that Ford has reduced Carter's lead to only 6 per cent.

October 22. A third presidential debate is held in Williamsburg, Virginnia. Both candidates are careful, polite and precise but the debating edge goes to Carter. Ford nonetheless predicts he will achieve the "political surprise of the century."

The Candidacy of Eugene McCarthy is ruled off the New York York State ballot, a decision of great importance considering Carter's narrow victory in that state.

October 23. Ford leaves Washington to begin his ten-day campaign windup. He launches a $4,000,000 media blitz and delivers five thirty minute speeches on TV before November 2.

October 25. Reagan begins a seven state Western tour for

Ford. Dole blames the Democrats for America's four twentieth century wars, a charge he later repudiates.

The British pound falls to its lowest point in history, $1.595.

October 26. Ten Nobel Prize winners accuse Ford of "inaccurate" claims about his administration's support of scientific research.

The Court of Appeals rules that tapes of Richard Nixon's Oval Office conversations may be reproduced and sold to the public. The Nixon issue may have weighed decisively against the Ford campaign.

October 27. At Villanova University, Ford harshly attacks Nixon's "imperial White House, " stating that "personal integrity is not too much to ask from a public official. "

Treasury officials reveal that the United States spent $11.4 billion less than expected from January through September; this underexpenditure caused the "pause" in the economy that may have cost Ford the election.

October 28. Ford orders the sale to China of computers with atomic technology capability.

October 29. Although the index of leading indicators declines for the second consecutive month and lower GNP growth rates confirm the "pause, " the stock market is again optimistic and advances twenty-six points in this last week before election. Ford has staged a major comeback by emphasizing his desire to hold down inflation, reduce taxes on the middle class, deregulate the oil industry and reduce the intrusiveness of government.

October 31. Four blacks attempt to attend services in Carter's church in Plains, Georgia, and services are cancelled.

November 1. The "black desk" of the Ford campaign sends telegrams to 400 black ministers detailing the Plains incident. Carter denounces the incident as politically motivated and the Ford Committee disavows its telegram.

November 2. One of the closest races in American political history is not decided until 4:00 A.M., when Mississippi

joins the Carter electoral total and gives him the election.
The result shows Carter with 297 electoral and 40,827,394
popular votes against 241 electoral and 39,145,977 popular
votes for Ford. In fourteen states the two candidates were
within 2 per cent of each other.

THE INTERREGNUM

November 4. Stock and bond prices drop in a gut reaction
to Carter's election, but in New York City a bond issue
finds buyers for the first time in a year.

The Rhodesian negotiations are threatened when nationa-
lists reject March 1, 1978, as the date for black majority
rule. Five "frontline" African states endorse guerilla war
on November 6, and the talks collapse completely in January,
1977.

November 5. The cabinet applauds Ford's declaration he
will govern until January 20. Despite his bravado, his
first electoral loss dampens the president's spirits for a month.

November 7. After 35,000 deaths and over fifty ceasefires,
peace comes to Lebanon. Syria prepares to assume full
peacekeeping duties and to collect all heavy weapons.

November 11. The Security Council unanimously deplores
Israeli settlements in occupied Arab territories. It de-
clares "invalid" the incorporation of East Jerusalem into
Israel.

November 12. The stock market continues to vote against
Carter; it has lost all but one session since the election and
ends the week at 927.69.

In Paris, the United States meets formally with Vietnam
but we veto their admission to the United Nations (November 15).

November 13. A burgeoning legislative scandal implicates
up to ninety congressmen who may have accepted illegal
gifts from an agent of the South Korean government.

November 14. Carter's church in Plains, Georgia, votes
to admit qualified blacks for membership.

November 15. Quebec elects a separatist government
which, at least rhetorically, raises the issue of secession
from Canada.

The swine flu innoculation program already far behind schedule and hampered by public skepticism, runs short of vaccine for children. There is no case of swine flu until November 23.

November 16. A loan of $300,000,000 to the Portutuese
government is reported. The U.S. also will participate
in a $1.5 billion consortium to help the government of
Mario Soares.

November 17. China sets off a four kiloton atomic blast;
fallout again reaches the U.S.

November 18. The Spanish Parliament votes itself out of
existence as that nation moves haltingly toward post-Franco
democracy.

November 19. General Motors signs an inflationary labor
pact with the United Auto Workers.

The State Court of Appeals invalidates the keystone of New
York City's financial recovery plan, and orders payment
of a billion dollars to bondholders.

November 21. America signs a ten year trade agreement
with Rumania.

November 22. Ford meets with Carter at the White House
and wins lavish praise for his cooperation with the transition of power.

UNESCO grants Israel full membership.

Mary Louise Smith, chairman of the Republican National
Committee, resigns.

November 24. George Bush announces he will resign as
director of the CIA on Inauguration Day.

November 28. International finance continues in chaos as
Australia devalues its currency and joins a list of troubled
nations which includes France, Britain, Japan, Mexico

and even Canada.

November 29. Big Steel announces its second major price increase in a year. The Ford administration implies that raised prices are unjustified and on December 2, advises consumers to bargain for discount prices.

November 30. Brezhnev, in a message to Carter, accuses the Ford administration of delaying a SALT II settlement due to election year politics. November unemployment reaches 8.1 per cent, the highest level of 1976.

December 1. Jose Lopez Portillo takes office as the new president of Mexico.

America abstains as Angola becomes the 146th member of the United Nations.

Ford places his Washington home on the market preparatory to his relocation in Southern California. On January 10, he receives his full asking price of $137,000.

December 2. Secretary Simon returns from Moscow with assurances that the Soviet Union will "go out of its way" to avoid challenging the incoming administration.

The Defense Department approves the $22.8 billion B-1 bomber program but gives Carter until June 1977, to decide whether it will be completely funded.

December 4. President Marcos of the Phillipines rejects a five-year, billion dollar base and economic aid agreement.

December 5. Japan's Liberal-Democratic Party, in large measure due to the Lockheed scandal, loses its electoral majority for the first time in twenty-one years.

December 6. A national debate on the death penalty is in progress as the Supreme Court, for the second time in three days, delays a scheduled execution.

December 8. Intelligence agencies charge that Attorney General Levi's reluctance to approve six wiretaps has hindered their counter espionage efforts. Greater concern for legal procedures is a clear result of the never-ending intelligence revelations of the Ford years.

December 9. Ford emerges from his isolation; he chairs
a meeting of Republican leaders which proposes a GOP
coordinating committee to keep "viable" our two party
system.

NATO follows Kissinger's advice and rejects a Soviet proposal to mutually renounce the first use of atomic weapons,
an indication of NATO fears of increasing Soviet tactical
strength.

The House approves new investigations into the assassinations of John F. Kennedy and Martin Luther King.

December 10. West Point cadets refuse to change the honor
system which resulted in the cheating scandal. However,
a commission, headed by former astronaut Frank Borman,
recommends readmission of all dismissed cadets (December 15).

December 14. Ford donates all papers from his twenty-
eight years in government service to the federal government; he asks they be preserved in a depository and museum in the state of Michigan. Philip Buchan says a national drive will be mounted in 1977 to finance a Ford
Library.

December 15. A plan to store up to 500 million barrels of
crude oil in salt dunes along the Gulf Coast is announced
by the administration.

December 16. The national swine flu program is suspended
after five persons die of Guillan-Baire Syndrome after being
innoculated. Fewer than 40 per cent of Americans received
immunization shots.

OPEC divides over the extent of a price increase in oil.
Saudi Arabis raises its price only 5 per cent but tells the
United States it expects Israeli concessions toward a per-
manent Mideastern peace.

Federal Court decides that Nixon, Mitchell and Haldeman
are liable for civil damages growing out of an illegal wire
tap that they approved.

December 19. A federal housing rehabilitation program is announced for New York City; it creates up to 1500 jobs by allowing contracting at 25 per cent below union wage scales.

Betty Ford receives her first college degree, an Ll. D from Michigan.

December 20. The UN General Assembly endorses black "armed struggle" in southwest Africa; the United States is one of only six nations to oppose the resolution.

Israeli Prime Minister Rabin resigns and calls elections for the spring.

Kissinger announces his official papers will be donated to the Library of Congress. Since becoming secretary of state in September, 1973, he has visited fifty-seven nations in forty international journeys covering 560,000 miles.

December 21. The Liberian freighter Argo Merchant splits apart off Nantucket and causes the worst oil spill in our history. This is the first in a series of tanker accidents that bring the year to a close and indicate our continued reliance on imported oil.

December 23. Carter completes selection of a rather unexciting Cabinet, all of whom win Senate approval.

December 24. Takeo Fukuda becomes prime minister of Japan.

December 26. The Air Force awards an evaluation contract for the Sparrow missile to Raytheon Corporation, which built the Sparrow. Rumsfeld defends the decision as essentially proper (January 7).

Senator Philip Hart, "Conscience of the Senate," dies. His widow asks Ford to pardon all Vietnam draft resisters but the president decides he cannot do so.

December 27. USDA admits overpayments of $215,000,000 in the food stamp program from January to June, 1976.

December 28. For "foreign policy reasons," Ford rejects CAB proposals which would have granted eleven metropolitan areas their first trans-Atlantic air routes.

December 31. Ford shocks America by proposing that
Puerto Rico become the fifty-first state, a decision made
without consultation and in violation of the principle of
self-determination.

The Dow Jones stock index ends the year at 1004.65, up
forty-nine points in December and a 16 per cent gain for
the year. Despite a trade deficit of $5.9 billion, it has
been a generally successful economic year. Ford's primary economic goal is attained as the inflation rate is only
4.8 per cent, the best in four years. His greatest economic failure is the persistence of high unemployment.

1977   January 1. Chief Justice Burger's report on the Judiciary
attacks wide sentencing disparities and calls once again
for higher judicial salaries. Ford does recommend higher
federal salaries before he leaves office.

January 2. ABC televises an interview Ford granted on
December 4. He says his greatest achievement was re-
storing trust in government; his toughest decision was the
Mayaguez rescue; and his greatest failure the inability
"to turn the economy around."

Governor Carlos Romero Barcelo, of Puerto Rico, ignores
Ford's suggestion of statehood while delivering his Inaugural Address.

January 3. The IMF grants Great Britain $3.9 billion in
credits.

January 4. Simon refuses New York City's claim for
$2,000,000 in costs for protecting UN diplomats, this
despite the understood intention of the law of December
31, 1975. Secretary Coleman, however, fulfills Ford's
pledge and approves construction of Westway.

Ford resurrects his October 1975, proposal of a permanent $10 billion cut in taxes and higher social security taxes.

January 5. Army Secretary Martin Hoffman rejects the
Borman Commission proposals and decides that expelled
cadets can reenter West Point only after a year's suspen-
sion.

Ford chairs a meeting of Republican leaders, but they fail

to agree on a new national chairman.

January 6. Congress formally counts the electoral vote:
Carter - 297, Ford - 240, Reagan - 1.

January 7. Ford sends a final energy message to Congress
and once again demands action to obtain "an adequate and
secure supply of energy at reasonable prices." The stalemate on energy policy is one of the great failures of his
administration. On January 11, Ford recommends creation
of a cabinet level department of energy.

January 10. Kissinger says that the very idea of military
supremacy in the modern nuclear age is foolish, a position
that radically opposes him to Rumsfeld, the Pentagon and
the CIA. Ford's inability to complete the SALT II talks
must be judged a major dispppointment of his administration.

January 11. The Justice Department announces it will not
prosecute Howard Callaway.

The Supreme Court decides that suburban zoning codes
need not be altered even if the practical effect is to block
the construction of integrated, low and middle income
housing projects.

January 12. Ford delivers a valedictory State of the Union
Message. "There is room for improvement as always, but
today we have a more perfect union than when my stewardship began."

January 13. Syria's collection of heavy armaments from the
PLO and others in Lebanon is concluded, but the future
remains cloudy for that troubled land.

January 14. Ex-Senator William Brock is selected as a
compromise national chairman for the GOP.

January 15. A Gallup Poll reports that most Americans
consider Ford an "average" president who restored confidence in American institutions, a not unworthy claim on
history.

January 17. Gary Gilmore, a thirty-six year old murderer,
becomes the first man to be executed in the United States

since 1967, a sentence carried out only after four stays of execution and two suicide attempts.

Ford sends Congress a fiscal 1978 budget of $440 billion, which includes a deficit of $47 billion. It is a document certain to be ignored by Congress and the new Carter administration.

A harbor crash in Barcelona kills at least forty-six American sailors.

January 18. Prime Minister Ghandi of India unexpectedly calls national elections for March.

HEW accuses NYC of discriminatory practices against minority and female teachers. Ford's attempts to deal with the issues of desegregation by attacking only the busing issue, constitute a serious failure of his leadership.

Ford again asks Congress to approve the March, 1976, base agreement with Turkey.

January 19. Ford pardons some 700 Vietnam veterans who received wounds or decorations but later left the services with less than honorable discharges. He also pardons "Tokyo Rose."

An executive order ends price controls on gasoline, an order rescinded by Carter on January 24.

The federal EPA bans the discharge of PCB into U.S. waters.

The Dow Jones ends the Ford administration registering 968.67.

January 20. James Earl Carter takes the oath as thirty-ninth president of the United States and thanks Ford for "healing our land."

January 21. As Ford participates in a celebrity golf tournament, Carter grants a full pardon to Vietnam draft evaders. Not a total amnesty, it applies only to some 10,000 men. The pardon is condemned by veterans groups and resisters alike. Thus, like Ford's, the Carter administration begins with a battle over a pardon.

January 30. NBC announces that Ford has signed a long-term contract to appear on documentaries about the presidency. Ford has also agreed to become president of the Eisenhower Exchange Fellowships (February 1) and the chairman of the board of the Academy for Educational Development (March 1).

February 7. While serving as Chubb Fellow at Yale, Ford blames a "logistics problem" for his famous snub of Solzhenitsyn. He claims America's "motives were right" all through the Vietnam debacle.

March 9. Ford and his wife sign million dollar contracts to write their memoirs.

March 15. Congress accepts Ford's decision to cancel the fourth Nimitz class nuclear carrier.

March 24. Ford consults with Carter in the Oval Office.

April 11. In a speech at Lexington, Kentucky, the former president asserts that in the six major crises of his presidency it was logistically impossible to consult with Congress. He urges re-examination of the War Powers Resolution of 1973.

DOCUMENTS

The first twenty-five years of Gerald Ford's public career were spent in the clubby confines of the House of Representatives, where he rose to the position of minority leader. Ford was hardworking, friendly and made no enemies; he was the living embodiment of the old saw "to get along, go along," while he ably serviced the needs of both his Michigan constituency and the Republican Party. He built a career on his solid character, his party loyalty and his belief in a strong defense establishment. Pursuing his cherished hope of someday being speaker of the House, Ford travelled extensively to campaign for G.O.P. candidates in marginal districts and preached solid conservative Republicanism to America. Yet despite all of his efforts, and in the face of two Nixon presidential victories, Republican strength in the House continued to decline and a dispirited Ford intended to retire to the quiet practice of law and lobbying.

Ford's planned retirement was aborted by the scandal which ultimately resulted in the resignation of Vice President Spiro T. Agnew. On October 12, 1973 Nixon introduced Ford to the nation as his new choice for vice president. As the honored guests and his congressional colleagues cheered, Ford remarked to the president, "I have a couple of friends out there." In truth, his beliefs and his honesty were well known after twelve House terms, and although the hearings that preceded Ford's elevation to the vice presidency were quite through, no observer seriously doubted there outcome. Whether Richard Nixon's supposed disdain of the minority leader led him to believe that the prospect of a Ford presidency could prevent his impeachment may never be known. However, even in 1973, some congressmen believed they were questioning the next president.

Ford served only eight months in his new office before the Watergate scandal took him to the Oval Office. The candor and the style with which Ford coped with his awesome and unexpected responsibilities are made evident in the documents that follow. Illustrative of both the strengths and the weaknesses of Ford, they summarize his philosophy of government and his dreams for America.

FORD BECOMES PRESIDENT
AUGUST 9, 1974

Just as Ford rose to the vice presidency under
the terms of the Constitution, so did the inex-
orable processes of the law destroy the presidency of Richard Nixon. The Watergate scandal, the most awesome political struggle in
American history, ultimately forced the resignation of the president of the United States.
Gerald R. Ford, the accidental vice-president,
became president of the United States at 12:03
P.M. on August 9, 1974. His appeal for
"straight talk among friends" and his dedication to the Constitution reassured the nation
and set it on the path toward healing.

Source: White House Press Release,
August 9, 1974

Mr. Chief Justice, my dear friends, my fellow Americans:

The oath that I have taken is the same oath that was taken by George
Washington and by every President under the Constitution. But I assume
the Presidency under extraordinary circumstances, never before experienced by Americans. This is an hour of history that troubles our minds
and hurts our hearts.

Therefore, I feel it is my first duty to make an unprecedented com-
pact with my countrymen. Not an inaugural address, not a fireside chat,
not a campaign speech. Just a little straight talk among friends. And I
intend it to be the first of many.

I am acutely aware that you have not elected me as your President
by your ballots, and so I ask you to confirm me as your President with
your prayers. And I hope that such prayers will also be the first of many.

If you have not chosen me by secret ballot, neither have I gained office by any secret promises. I have not campaigned either for the Presidency or the Vice Presidency. I have not subscribed to any partisan platform. I am indebted to no man, and only to one woman -- my dear wife
--as I begin this very difficult job.

I have not sought this enormous responsibility, but I will not shirk it.
Those who nominated me and confirmed me as Vice President were my
friends and are my friends. They were of both parties, elected by all the
people and acting under the Constitution in their name. It is only fitting
then that I should pledge to them and to you that I will be the President of
all the people.

Thomas Jefferson said the people are the only sure reliance for the preservation of our liberty. And down the years, Abraham Lincoln renewed this American article of faith asking, "Is there any better way or equal hope in the world?"

I intend, on Monday next, to request of the Speaker of the House of Representatives and the President pro tempore of the Senate the privilege of appearing before the Congress to share with my former colleagues and with you, the American people, my views on the priority business of the Nation and to solicit your views and their views. And may I say to the Speaker and the others, if I could meet with you right after these remarks, I would appreciate it.

Even though this is late in an election year, there is no way we can go forward except together and no way anybody can win except by serving the people's urgent needs. We cannot stand still or slip backwards. We must go forward now together.

To the peoples and the governments of all friendly nations, and I hope that could encompass the whole world, I pledge an uninterrupted and sincere search for peace. America will remain strong and united, but its strength will remain dedicated to the safety and sanity of the entire family of man, as well as to our own precious freedom.

I believe that truth is the glue that holds Government together, not only our Government, but civilization itself. That bond, though strained, is unbroken at home and abroad.

In all my public and private acts as your President, I expect to follow my instincts of openness and candor with full confidence that honesty is always the best policy in the end.

My fellow Americans, our long national nightmare is over.

Our Constitution works; our great Republic is a Government of laws and not of men. Here the people rule. But there is a higher power, by whatever name we honor Him, who ordains not only rightousness but love, not only justice but mercy.

As we bind up the internal wounds of Watergate, more painful and more poisonous than those of foreign wars, let us restore the golden rule to our political process, and let brotherly love purge our hearts of suspicion and of hate.

In the beginning, I asked you to pray for me. Before closing, I ask again your prayers, for Richard Nixon and for his family. May our former President, who brought peace to millions, find it for himself. May God bless and comfort his wonderful wife and daughters, whose love and loyalty will forever be a shining legacy to all who bear the lonely burdens of the White House.

I can only guess at those burdens, although I have witnessed at close hand the tragedies that befell three Presidents and the lesser trials of others....

God helping me, I will not let you down.

ADDRESS TO THE CONGRESS
AUGUST 12, 1974

As the "burdens" of the presidency fell on
Ford, he moved to reassure the nation
that there would be continuity of policy; he
went out of his way to emphasize that
foreign policy would remain the purview
of Secretary Kissinger. On the evening
of August 12, he spoke to Congress and
identified the major crisis facing the nation - the spectre of run-away inflation.
There was no doubt that Americans wished
our "nightmare" to end and the first month
of Ford's presidency was a period of eu-
phoria as the nation sought to regain its
lost confidence.

Source: White House Press Release,
August 12, 1974.

I am not here to make an inaugural address. The Nation needs action,
not words. Nor will this be a formal report on the State of the Union.
God willing, I will have at least three more chances to do that.

It is good to be back in the People's House. But this cannot be a real
homecoming. Under the Constitution, I now belong to the Executive Branch.
The Supreme Court has even ruled that I am the Executive Branch, head,
heart, and hand....

This Congress, unless it has changed, I am confident, will be my
working partner as well as my most constructive critic. I am not asking
for conformity. I am dedicated to the two-party system, and you know
which party I belong to.

I do not want a honeymoon with you. I want a good marriage.

I want progress and I want problem-solving which requires my best
efforts, and also your best efforts.

I have no need to learn how Congress speaks for the people. As President, I intend to listen.

But I also intend to listen to the people themselves -- all the people --
as I promised last Friday. I want to be sure that we are all tuned in to the
real voice of America.

My Administration starts off by seeking unity in diversity. My office
door has always been open, and that is how it is going to be at the White
House. Yes, Congressmen will be welcomed -- if you don't overdo it.
(Laughter)

The first seven words of the Constitution and the most important are these: We the people of the United States. We, the people, ordained and established the Constitution and reserved to themselves all powers not granted to Federal and State Governments. I respect and will always be conscious of that fundamental rule of freedom.

Only eight months ago, when I last stood here, I told you I was a Ford, not a Lincoln. Tonight I say I am still a Ford, but I am not a Model T.

I do have some old fashioned ideas, however. I believe in the very basic decency and fairness of America. I believe in the integrity and patriotism of the Congress. And while I am aware of the House rule that no one ever speaks to the galleries, I believe in the First Amendment and the absolute necessity of a free press.

But I also believe that over two centuries since the First Continental Congress was first convened, the direction of our Nation's movement has been forward. I am here to confess that in my first campaign for President -- of my senior class in South High School in Grand Rapids, Michigan -- I headed the Progressive Party ticket, and lost. Maybe that is why I became a Republican. (Laughter)

Now I ask you to join with me in getting this country revved up and moving.

My instinctive judgment is that the State of the Union is excellent. But the state of our economy is not so good. Everywhere I have been as Vice President, some 118,000 miles in 40 States and some 55 press conferences, the unanimous concern of Americans is inflation.

For once all the polls seem to agree. They also suggest that the people blame Government far more than either management or labor or for the high cost of everything they have to buy.

You who come from 50 States, three territories, and the District of Columbia, know this better than I do. That is why you have created, since I left, your new Budget Reform Committee. I welcome it, and I will work with it members to bring the Federal budget into balance in fiscal year 1976....

Just as escalating Federal spending has been a prime cause of higher prices over many years, it may take some time to stop inflation. But we must begin right now.

For a start, before your Labor Day recess, Congress should reactivate the Cost of Living Council through passage of a clean bill, without reimposing controls, that will let us monitor wages and prices to expose abuses.

Whether we like it or not, the American wage earner and the American housewife are a lot better economists than most economists care to admit. They know that a Government big enough to give you everything you want, is a Government big enough to take from you everything you have.

If we want to restore confidence in ourselves as working politicians, the first thing we all have to do is to learn to say, "No."

The first specific request by the Ford Administration is not to Congress but to the voters in the upcoming November election. It is this, very simple: Support your candidates, Congressmen and Senators, Democrats or Republicans, conservatives or liberals, who consistently vote for tough decisions to cut the cost of Government, restrain Federal spending and bring inflation under control....

My first priority is to work with you to bring inflation under control. Inflation is domestic enemy number one. To restore economic confidence, the Government in Washington must provide some leadership. It does no good to blame the public for spending too much when the Government is spending too much.

I began to put my Administration's own economic house in order starting last Friday.

I instructed my Cabinet officers and counsellors and my White House staff to make fiscal restraint their first order of business, and to save every taxpayer's dollar the safety and genuine welfare of our great Nation will permit. Some economic activities will be affected more by monetary and fiscal restraint than other activities. Good government clearly requires that we tend to the economic problems facing our country in a spirit of equity to all of our citizens in all segments of our society.

Tonight, obviously, is no time to threaten you with vetoes. But I do have the last recourse, and I am a veteran of many a veto fight right here in the great chamber. Can't we do a better job by reasonable compromise? I hope we can.

Minutes after I took the Presidential oath, the joint leadership of Congress told me at the White House they would go more than half way to meet me. This was confirmed in your unanimous concurrent resolution of cooperation, for which I am deeply grateful. If, for my part, I go more than half way to meet the Congress, maybe we can find a much larger area of national agreement.

I bring no legislative shipping list here this evening. I will deal with specifics in future messages and talks with you, but here are a few examples of how seriously I feel about what we must do together.

Last week, the Congress passed the elementary and secondary education bill, and I found it on my desk. Any reservations I might have about some of its provisions -- and I do have -- fade in comparison to the urgent needs of America for quality education. I will sign it in a few days.

I must be frank. In implementing its provisions, I will oppose excessive funding during this inflationary crisis.

As Vice President, I studied various proposals for better health care financing. I saw them coming closer together and urged my friends in the Congress and in the Administration to sit down and sweat out a sound compromise. The Comprehensive Health Insurance Plan goes a long ways toward providing early relief to people who are sick.

Why don't we write -- and I ask this with the greatest spirit of cooperation -- why don't we write a good health bill on the statute books in 1974, before this Congress adjourns.

The economy of our country is critically dependent on how we interact with the economies of other countries. It is little comfort that our inflation is only a part of a world-wide problem, or that American families need less of their paychecks for groceries that most of our foreign friends.

As one of the building blocks of peace, we have taken the lead in working toward a more open and more equitable world economic system. A new round of international trade negotiations started last September among 105 nations in Tokyo. The others are waiting for the United States Congress to grant the necessary authority to the Executive branch to proceed.

With modification, the trade reform bill passed by the House last year would do a good job. I understand good progress has been made in the Senate Committee on Finance. But I am optimistic as always that the Senate will pass an acceptable bill quickly as a key part of our joint prosperity campaign.

I am determined to expedite other international economic plans. We will be working together with other nations to find better ways to prevent shortages of food and fuel. We must not let last winter's energy crisis happen again. I will push Project Independence for our own good and the good of others. In that, too, I will need your help.

Successful foreign policy is an extension of the hopes of the whole American people for a world of peace and orderly reform and orderly freedom. So, I would say a few words to our distinguished guests from the governments of other nations, where, as at home, it is my determination to deal openly with allies and adversaries.

Over the past five and one-half years in Congress, and as Vice President, I have fully supported the outstanding foreign policy of President Nixon. This policy I intend to continue ••••

We stand by our commitments and we will live up to our responsibilities, in our formal alliances, in our friendships, and in our improving relations with potential adversaries.

On this, Americans are united and strong. Under my term of leadership, I hope we will become more united. I am certain America will remain strong.

A strong defense is the surest way to peace. Strength makes detente attainable. Weakness invites war as my generation, my generation knows from four very bitter experiences.

Just as America's will for peace is second to none, so will America's strength be second to none.

We cannot rely on the forebearance of others to protect this Nation. The power and diversity of the Armed Forces, active guard and reserve, the resolve of our fellow citizens, the flexibility in our command to navigate international waters that remain troubled, are all essential to our security.

I shall continue to insist on civilian control of our superb military establishment. The Constitution plainly requires the President to be Commander-in-Chief and I will be.

Our job will not be easy. In promising continuity, I cannot promise simplicity. The problems and challenges of the world remain complex and difficult. But we have set out on a path of reason, of fairness, and we will continue on it.

To all nations, I pledge continuity in seeking a common global goal, a stable international structure of trade and finance which reflects the interdependence of all peoples.

To the entire international community -- to the United Nations, to the world's non-aligned nations, and to all others -- I pledge continuity in our dedication to the humane goals which throughout our history have been so much of America's contribution to mankind.

So long as the peoples of the world have confidence in our purposes and faith in our word, the age-old vision of peace on earth grows brighter.

I pledge myself unreservedly to that goal. I say to you in words that cannot be improved upon: Let us never negotiate out of fear, but let us never fear to negotiate.

As Vice President, at the request of the President, I addressed myself to the individual rights of Americans in the area of privacy. There will be no illegal tappings, eavesdripping, buggings, or break-ins by my Administration. There will be hot pursuit of tough laws to prevent illegal invasion of privacy in both Government and private activities.

On the higher plane of public morality, there is no need for me to preach tonight. We have thousands of far better preachers and millions of sacred scriptures to guide us on the path of personal right-living and exemplary official conduct. If we can make effective and earlier use of moral and ethical wisdom of the centuries in today's complex society, we will prevent more crime and more corruption than all the policemen and prosecutors governments can ever deter. If I may say so, this is a job that must begin at home, not in Washington.

I once told you that I am not a saint, and I hope never to see the day that I cannot admit having made a mistake, so I will close with another confession.

Frequently, along the tortuous road of recent months from this chamber to the President's House, I protested that I was my own man. Now I realize that I was wrong.

I am your man, for it was your carefully weighed confirmation that changed my occupation.

The truth is I am the people's man, for you acted in their name, and I accepted and began my new and solemn trust with a promise to serve all the people and do the best that I can for America.

When I say all the people, I mean exactly that.

To the limits of my strength and ability, I will be the President of black, brown, red and white Americans, of old and young, of women's liberationists and male chauvinists (Laughter) and all the rest of us in between, of the poor and the rich, of native sons and new refugees, of those who work at lathes or at desks or in mines or in the fields, or of

Christians, Jews, Moslems, Buddhists and Atheists, if there really are any Atheists after what we have all been through.

Fellow Americans, one final word:

I want to be a good President.

I need your help.

We all need God's sure guidance.

With it, nothing can stop the United States of America.

FORD PARDONS NIXON
SEPTEMBER 9, 1974

Although the Clemency Board created by Ford
in September, 1974 was never fully accepted by
either veterans or deserters, its existence illustrated the president's desire to break with the
past. He nominated Nelson Rockefeller to be his
vice president on August 20, presided over the
opening of the Conference on Inflation on September 5, and generally received rhapsodic press
coverage. The spirit of America soared until
Sunday morning, September 8, when Ford announced his pardon of Richard Nixon. Allegations of "deal" were immediately heard, and
though never substantiated, cast a never lifting shadow across the entire Ford presidency.

Source: White House Press Release,
September 8, 1974 and "Proclamation of Pardon,"
New York Times, September 9, 1974.

Ladies and gentlemen, I have come to a decision which I felt I should
tell you and all of my fellow American citizens, as soon as I was certain
in my own mind and in my own conscience that it is the right thing to do.

I have learned already in this office that the difficult decision always
come to this desk. I must admit that many of them do not look at all the
same as the hypothetical questions that I have answered freely and perhaps too fast on previous occasions.

My customary policy is to try and get all the facts and to consider the
opinions of my countrymen and to take counsel with my most valued friends.
But these seldom agree, and in the end, the decision is mine. To procras-
tinate, to agonize and to wait for a more favorable turn of events that may
never come, or more compelling external pressures that may as well be
wrong as right, is itself a decision of sorts, and a weak and potentially
dangerous course for a President to follow.

I have promised to uphold the Constitution, to do what is right as God
gives me to see the right, and to do the very best that I can for America.

I have asked your help and your prayers, not only when I became
President, but many times since. The Constitution is the supreme law of
our land and it governs our actions as citizens. Only the laws of God,
which govern our consciences, are superior to it.

As we are a nation under God, so I am sworn to uphold our laws with
the help of God. And I have sought such guidance and searched my own
conscience with special diligence to determine the right thing for me to do

with respect to my predecessor in this place, Richard Nixon, and his
loyal wife and family.

Theirs is an American tragedy in which we all have played a part.
It could go on and on and on, or someone must write the end to it. I have
concluded that only I can do that, and if I can, I must.

There are no historic or legal precedents to which I can turn in this
matter, none that precisely fit the circumstances of a private citizen who
has resigned the Presidency of the United States. But it is common knowledge that serious allegations and accusations hang like a sword over our
former President's head, threatening his health as he tries to reshape his
life, a great part of which was spent in the service of this country and by
the mandate of its people.

After years of bitter controversy and divisive national debate, I have
been advised, and I am compelled to conclude that many months and perhaps more years will have to pass before Richard Nixon could obtain a
fair trial by jury in any jurisdiction of the United States under governing
decisions of the Supreme Court.

I deeply believe in equal justice for all Americans, whatever their
station or former station. The law, whether human or devine, is no respecter of persons, but the law is a respecter of reality.

The facts, as I see them are that a former President of the United
States, instead of enjoying equal treatment with any other citizen accused
of violating the law, would be cruelly and excessively penalized either in
preserving the presumption of his innocence or in obtaining a speedy determination of his guilt in order to repay a legal debt to society.

During this long period of delay and potential litigation, ugly passions
would again be aroused. And our people would again be polarized in their
opinions. And the credibility of our free institutions of Government would
again be challenged at home and abroad.

In the end, the courts might well hold that Richard Nixon had been
denied due process and the verdict of history would even more be incon-
clusive with respect to those charges arising out of the period of his
Presidency, of which I am presently aware.

But it is not the ultimate fate of Richard Nixon that most concerns me,
though surely it deeply troubles every decent and every compassionate
person. My concern is the immediate future of this great country.

In this, I dare not depend upon my personal sympathy as a long-time
friend of the former President, nor my professional judgment as a lawyer,
and I do not.

As President, my primary concern must always be the greatest good
of all the people of the United States whose servant I am. As a man, my
first consideration is to be true to my own convictions and my own conscience.

My conscience tells me clearly and certainly that I cannot prolong the
bad dreams that continue to reopen a chapter that is closed. My conscience tells me that only I, as President, have the constitutional power

to firmly shut and seal this book. My conscience tells me it is my duty, not merely to proclaim domestic tranquility, but to use every means that I have to insure it.

I do believe that the buck stops here, that I cannot rely upon public opinion polls to tell me what is right.

I do believe that right makes might, and that if I am wrong, ten angels swearing I was right would make no difference.

I do believe, with all my heart and mind and spirit, that I, not as President, but as a humble servant of God, will receive justice without mercy if I fail to show mercy.

Finally, I feel that Richard Nixon and his loved ones have suffered enough and will continue to suffer, no matter what I do, no matter what we, as a great and good Nation, can do together to make his goal of peace come true. . . .

PROCLAMATION OF PARDON

Richard Nixon became the thirty-seventh President of the United States on January 20, 1969, and was re-elected in 1972 for a second term by the electors of forty-nine of the fifty states. His term in office continued until his resignation on August 9, 1974.

Pursuant to resolutions of the House of Representatives, its Committee on the Judiciary conducted an inquiry and investigation on the impeachment of the President extending over more than eight months. The hearings of the committee and its deliberations which received wide national publicity over television, radio, and in printed media, resulted in votes adverse to Richard Nixon on recommended Articles of Impeachment.

As a result of certain acts or omissions occurring before his resignation from the office of President, Richard Nixon has become liable to possible indictment and trial for offenses against the United States. Whether or not he shall be so prosecuted depends on findings of the appropriate grand jury and on the discretion of the authorized prosecutor. Should an indictment ensue, the accused shall then be entitled to a fair trial by an impartial jury, as guaranteed to every individual by the Constitution.

It is believed that a trial of Richard Nixon, if it became necessary, could not fairly begin until a year or more has elapsed. In the meantime, the tranquility to which this nation has been restored by the events of recent weeks could be irreparably lost by the prospects of bringing to trial a former President of the United States. The prospects of such a trial will cause prolonged and divisive debate over

the propriety of exposing to further punishment and degra-
dation a man who has already paid the unprecedented penalty of relinquishing the highest elective office in the
United States.

NOW, THEREFORE, I, Gerald R. Ford, President of
the United States, pursuant to the pardon power conferred
upon me by Article II, Section 2, of the Constitution, have
granted and by these presents do grant a full, free, and
absolute pardon unto Richard Nixon for all offenses against
the United States which he, Richard Nixon, has committed
or may have committed or taken part in during the period
from January 20, 1969, through August 9, 1974.

IN WITNESS WHEREOF, I have hereunto set my hand
this 8th day of September in the year of our Lord nineteen
hundred seventy-four, and of the independence of the United
States of America the 199th.

ADDRESS TO THE CONGRESS - THE "WIN" CAMPAIGN,
OCTOBER 8, 1974

During the first six weeks of the Ford administration, a series of twenty-four conferences were held to organize a strategy
against "the nation's number one problem, "
inflation. The president himself spoke at
the opening and concluding sessions of the
culminating conference on September 27-28.
Yet despite the most vigorous efforts, the
American economy continued to slip into its
worse recession since World War II. The
stock market hit a twelve year low and the
leading economic indicators showed only
depressing figures. The president stitched
together the many suggestions that had been
made and on October 8, he presented to the
American people his plan to "Whip Inflation
Now. "

Source: White House Press Release,
October 8, 1974

In his first inaugural address, President Franklin Roosevelt said, and
I quote: "The people of the United States have not failed. . .They want direct, vigorous action, and they have asked for discipline and direction under our leadership. "

Today, though our economic difficulties do not approach the emergency
of 1933, the message from the American people is exactly the same. I
trust that you are getting the very same message that I am receiving: Our
constituents want leadership, our constituents want action.

All of us have heard much talk on this very floor about Congress recovering its rightful share of national leadership. I now intend to offer
you that chance. . . .

I will not take your time today with the discussion of the origins of inflation and its bad effect on the United States, but I do know where we want
to be in 1976 on the 200th birthday of a United States of America that has
not lost its way, nor its will, nor its sense of national purpose.

During the meetings on inflation, I listened carefully to many valuable
suggestions. Since the summit, I have evaluated literally hundreds of ideas,
day and night.

My conclusions are very simply stated. There is only one point on
which all advisers have agreed: We must whip inflation right now.

None of the remedies proposed, great or small, compulsory or volun-

tary, stands a chance unless they are combined in a considered package,
in a concerted effort, in a grand design.

I have reviewed the past and the present efforts of our Federal Government to help the economy. They are simply not good enough, nor sufficiently broad, nor do they pack the punch that will turn America's economy
on.

A stable American economy cannot be sustained if the world's economy
is in chaos. International cooperation is abolutely essential and vital, but
while we seek agreements with other nations, let us put our own economic
house in order.

Today, I have identified ten areas for our joint action, the Executive
and the Legislative Branches of our Government.

Number One: Food.

America is the world's champion producer of food. Food prices and
petroleum prices in the United States are primary inflationary factors.

America today partially depends on foreign sources for petroleum,
but we can grow more than enough food for ourselves.

To halt higher food prices, we must produce more food, and I call
upon every farmer to produce the full capacity. And I say to you and to
the farmers, they have done a magnificent job in the past, and we should
be eternally grateful.

This Government, however, will do all in its power to assure him, that
farmer, he can sell his entire yield at reasonable prices. Accordingly,
I ask the Congress to remove all remaining acreage limitations on rice,
peanuts, and cotton.

I also assure America's farmer here and now that I will allocate all
the fuel and ask authority to allocate all the fertilizer they need to do this
essential job. . . .

Number Two: Energy.

America's future depends heavily on oil, gas, coal, electricity, and
other resources called energy. Make no mistake, we do have a real energy
problem.

One-third of our oil -- 17 percent of America's total energy -- now
comes from foreign sources that we cannot control, at high cartel prices
costing you and me $16 billion -- $16 billion more than just a year ago.

A primary solution has to be at home. If you have forgotten the shortages of last winter, most Americnns have not.

I have ordered today the reorganization of our national energy effort
in the creation of a National Energy Board. It will be chaired with developing, or I should say charged with developing a single national energy policy
and program. And I think most of you will be glad to know that our former
colleague, Rog Morton, our Secretary of Interior, will be the overall boss
of our national energy program.

Rog Morton's marching orders are to reduce imports of foreign oil by
one million barrels per day by the end of 1975, whether by savings here at
home, or by increasing our own sources.

Secretary Morton, along with his other responsibility, is also charged with increasing our domestic energy supply by promptly utilizing our coal resources and expanding recovery of domestic oil still in the grounds in old wells.

New legislation will be sought after your recess to require use of cleaner coal processes and nuclear fuel in new electric plants and the quick conversion of existing oil plants.

I propose that we, together, set a target date of 1980 for eliminating oil-fired plants from the Nation's base-loaded electrical capacity.

I will use the Defense Production Act to allocate scarce materials for energy development, and I will ask you, the House and Senate, for whatever amendments prove necessary.

I will meet with top management of the automobile industry to assure, either by agreement or by law, a firm program aimed at achieving a 40 percent increase in gasoline mileage within a four-year development deadline.

Priority legislation -- action, I should say -- to increase energy supply here at home requires the following:

One, long-sought deregulation of natural gas supplies.

Number two, responsible use of our Naval petroleum reserves in California and Alaska.

Number three, amendments to the Clean Air Act, and

Four, passage of surface mining legislation to insure an adequate supply with common-sense environmental protection.

Now, if all of these steps fail to meet our current energy saving goals, I will not hestitate to ask for tougher measure. For the long range, we must work harder on coal gasification. We must push with renewed vigor and talent research in the use of nonfossil fuels. The power of the atom, the heat of the sun and the steam stored deep in the earth, the force of the winds and water, must be main sources of energy for our grandchildren, and we can do it.

Number Three: Restrictive Practices.

To increase productivity and contain prices, we must end restrictive and costly practices, whether instituted by Government, industry, labor or others. And I am determined to return to the vigorous enforcement of antitrust laws. . . .

The Council on Wage and Price Stability will, of course, monitor wage and price increases in the private sector. Monitoring will include public hearings to justify either price or wage increases. I emphasize, in fact re-emphasize, that this is not a compulsory wage and price control agency.

Now, I know many Americans see Federal controls as the answer, but I believe from past experience controls show us that they never really stop inflation, not the last time, not even during and immediately after World War II, when, as I recall, prices rose despite severe and enforceable wartime rationing.

Now, peacetime controls actually, we know from recent experience

create shortages, hamper production, stifle growth and limit jobs. I do
not ask for such powers, however politically tempting, as such a program
could cause the fixer and the black marketeer to flourish, while decent
citizens face empty shelves and stand in long waiting lines.

Number Four: We Need More Capital.

We cannot "eat up our seed corn." Our free enterprise system depends on orderly capital markets through which the savings of our people
become productively used. Today, our capital markets are in total disar-
ray. We must restore their vitality. Prudent monetary restraint is essential.

You and the American people should know, however, I have personally been assured by the Chairman of the Independent Federal Reserve Board,
that the supply of money and credit will expand sufficiently to meet the
needs of our economy and that in no event will a credit crunch occur.

The prime lending rate is going down. To help industry to buy more
machines and create more jobs, I am recommending a liberalized 10 percent investment tax credit. This credit should be especially helpful to cap-
tal-intensive industries, such as primary metals, public utilities, where
capacity shortages have developed.

I am asking Congress to enact tax legislation to provide that all divi-
dends on preferred stocks issued for cash be fully deductible by the issu-
ing company. This should bring in more capital, especially for energy-
producing utilities. It will also help other industries shift from debt to
equity, providing a sounder capital structure.

Capital gains tax legislation must be liberalized as proposed by the
tax reform bill currently before the Committee on Ways and Means. I
endorse this approach and hope that it will pass promptly.

Number Five: Helping The Casualties.

And this is a very important part of the overall speech. The Conference on Inflation made everybody even more aware of who is suffering
most from inflation. Foremost are those who are jobless through no fault
of their own.

Three weeks ago, I released funds which, with earlier actions, provide public service employment for some 170,000 who need work. I now
propose to the Congress a two-step program to augment this action.

First, 13 weeks of special unemployment insurance benefits would be
provided to those who have exhausted their regular and extended unemployment insurance benefits would be provided to those who have exhausted
their regular and extended unemployment insurance benefits, and 26 weeks
of special unemployment insurance benefits to those who qualify but are
not now covered by regular unemployment insurance programs.

Funding in this case would come from the general treasury, not from
taxes on employers, as is the case with the established unemployment
program.

Second, I ask the Congress to create a brand new Community Improvement Corps to provide work for the unemployed through short-term useful

work projects to improve, beautify and enhance the environment of our cities, our towns and our countryside.

This standby program would come alive whenever unemployment exceeds 6 percent nationally. It would be stopped when unemployment drops below 6 percent. Local labor markets would each qualify for grants whenever their unemployment rate exceeds 6.5 percent ....

Number Six: Stimulating Housing.

Without question, credit is the lifeblood of housing. The United States, unfortunately, is suffering the longest and the most severe housing recession since the end of World War II. Unemployment in the construction trades is twice the national average.

One of my first acts as President was to sign the Housing and Community Development Act of 1974. I have since concluded that still more help is needed, help that can be delivered very quickly and with minimum inflationary impact.

I urge the Congress to enact before recess additional legislation to make most home mortgages eligible for purchase by an agency of the Federal Government. As the law stands now, only FHA or VA home mortgages, one fifth of the total, are covered. . . .

Number Seven: Thrift Institutions.

Savings and loan and similar institutions are hard hit by inflation and high interest rates. They no longer attract, unfortunately, adequate deposits. The Executive Branch, in my judgment, must join with the Congress in giving critically-needed attention to the structure and the operation of our thrift institutions which now find themselves for the third time in eight years in another period of serious mortgage credit scarcity. . . .

Number Eight: International Interdependency.

The United States has a responsibility not only to maintain a healthy economy at home, but also to seek policies which compliment rather than disrupt the constructive efforts of others.

Essential to U.S. initiatives is the early passage of an acceptable trade reform bill . . . .

Number Nine: Federal Taxes and Spending.

To support programs, to increase production and share inflation-produced hardships, we need additional tax revenues. I am aware that any proposal for new taxes just four weeks before a national election is, to put it mildly, considered politically unwise. And I am frank to say that I have been earnestly advised to wait and talk about taxes anytime after November 5.

But I do say in sincerity that I will not play politics with America's future.

Our present inflation, to a considerable degree, comes from many years of enacting expensive programs without raising enough revenues to pay for them.

The truth is that 19 out of the 25 years I had the honor and the privilege to serve in this Chamber, the Federal Government ended up with

Federal deficits. That is not a very good batting average.

By now, almost everybody -- almost everybody else, I should say -- has stated my position on Federal gasoline taxes. This time I will do it myself. I am not -- emphasizing not -- asking you for any increase in gas taxes.

I am -- I am asking you to approve a one-year temporary tax sur- charge of 5 percent on corporate and upper-level individual incomes.

This would generally exclude from the surcharge those families with gross incomes below $15,000 a year. The estimated $5 billion in extra re- venue to be raised by this inflation-fighting tax should pay for the new programs I have recommended in this message.

I think, and I suspect each of you know, this is the acid test of our joint determination to whip inflation in America. I would not ask this if major loopholes were not now being closed by the Committee on Ways and Means' tax reform bill.

I urge you to join me before your recess, in addition to what I have said before, to join me by voting to set a target spending limit -- let me emphasize it -- a target spending limit of $300 billion for the Federal fiscal budget of 1975.

When Congress agrees to this spending target, I will submit a package of budget deferrals and recisions to meet this goal. I will do the tough job of designating for Congressional action on your return those areas which which I believe can and must be reduced.

These will be hard choices and everyone of you in this Chamber know it as well as I.

They will be hard choices, but no Federal agency, including the De- fense Department, will be untouchable. . . .

My fellow Americans, ten days ago I asked you to get things started by making a list of ten ways to fight inflation and save energy, to exchange your list with your neighbors, and to send me a copy.

I have personally read scores of the thousands of letters received at the White House, and incidentially, I have made my economic experts read some of them, too. We all benefitted, at least I did, and I thank each and every one of you for this cooperation.

Some of the good ideas from your home to mine have been cranked into the recommendations I have just made to the Congress and the steps I am taking as President to whip inflation right now. There were also firm warnings on what Government must not do, and I appreciated those, too.

Your best suggestions for voluntary restraint and self-discipline showed me that a great degree of patriotic determination and unanimity al- ready exist in this great land.

I have asked Congress for urgent specific actions it alone can take. I advised Congress of the initial steps that I am taking as President. Here is what only you can do: Unless every able American pitches in, Congress and I cannot do the job.

Winning our fight against inflation and waste involves total mobilization of America's greatest resources, the brains, the skills and the will power of the American people.

Here is what we must do, what each and every one of you can do. To help increase food and lower prices, grow more and waste less. To help save scarce fuel in the energy crisis, drive less, heat less. Every housewife knows almost exactly how much she spent for food last week. If you cannot spare a penny from your food budget -- and I know there are many -- surely you can cut the food that you waste by 5 per cent.

Every American motorist knows exactly how many miles he or she drives to work or to school every day and about how much mileage she or he runs up each year. If we all drive at least 5 per cent fewer miles, we can save almost unbelievably 250,000 barrels of foreign oil per day by the end of 1975.

Most of us can do better than 5 per cent by car pooling, taking the bus, riding bikes or just plain walking. We can save enough gas by self-discipline to meet our one million barrels per day goal....

There will be no big Federal bureaucracy set up for this crash program. Through the courtesy of such volunteers from the communication and media fields, a very simple enlistment form will appear in many of tomorrow's newspapers, along with a symbol of this new mobilization, which I am wearing on my lapel.

It bears the single word WIN. I think that tells it all. I will call upon every American to join in this massive mobilization and stick with it until we do win as a Nation and as a people.

Mr. Speaker and Mr. President, I stand on a spot hallowed by history. Many Presidents have come here many times to solicit, to scold, to flatter, to exhort the Congress to support them in their leadership.

Once in a great whlile Presidents have stood here and truly inspired the most skeptical and the most sophisticated audience of their co-equal partners in Government.

Perhaps once or twice in a generation is there such a Joint Session. I don't expect this one to be. Only two of my predecessors have come in person to call upon Congress for a declaration of war, and I shall not do that.

But I say to you, with all sincerity, that our inflation, our public enemy number one, will, unless whipped, destroy our country, our homes, our liberties, our property, and finally our national pride, as surely as any well-armed wartime enemy.

I concede there will be no sudden Pearl Harbor to shock us into unity and into sacrifice, but I think we have had enough early warnings. The time to intercept is right now. The time to intercept is almost gone.

My friends and former colleagues, will you enlist now? My friends and fellow Americans, will you enlist now? Together with discipline and determination, we will win.

THE STATE OF THE UNION,
JANUARY 15, 1975

The WIN campaign turned out to be a fiasco. Inflation continued even as the economy settled into
the worst recession in forty years. On January 13,
1975 the president reversed his economic policy
and declared a "simultaneous three-pronged campaign against recession, inflation and energy dependence. Two days later, in his State of the Union
message, Ford reassured America that another
Great Depression was not in prospect, although
the state of the union was "not good."

Source: White House Press Release,
January 15, 1975

Twenty-six years ago, a freshman Congressman, a young fellow,
with lots of idealism who was out to change the world, stood before Speaker
Sam Rayburn in the well of this House and solemnly swore to the same
oath you took yesterday. That is an unforgettable experience, and I congratulate you all.

Two days later, that same freshman sat in the back row as President
Truman, all charged up by his single-handed election victory, reported
as the Constitution requires on the State of the Union.

When the bipartisan applause stopped, President Truman said:

"I am happy to report to this Eighty-first Congress that the State of
the Union is good. Our Nation is better able than ever before to meet the
needs of the American people and to give them their fair chance in the pursuit of happiness. It is foremost among the nations of the world in the
search for peace."

Today, that freshman Member from Michigan stands where Mr. Truman stood and I must say to you that the State of the Union is not good.

Millions of Americans are out of work. Recession and inflation are
eroding the money of millions more. Prices are too high and sales are
too slow.

This year's Federal deficit will be about $30 billion; next year's pro-
bably $45 billion. The national debt will rise to over $600 billion.

Our plant capacity and productivity are not increasing fast enough.
We depend on others for essential energy.

Some people question their government's ability to make the hard
decisions and stick with them. They expect Washington politics as usual.

Yet, what President Truman said on January 5, 1949, is even more
true in 1975.

We are better able to meet the peoples' needs.

All Americans do have a fairer chance to pursue happiness. Not only are we still the foremost nation in pursuit of peace, but today's prospects of attaining it are infinitely brighter.

There were 59,000,000 Americans employed at the start of 1949. Now there are more than 85,000,000 Americans who have jobs. In comparable dollars, the average income of the American family has doubled during the past 26 years.

Now, I want to speak very bluntly. I've got bad news, and I don't expect any applause. The American people want action and it will take both the Congress and the President to give them what they want. Progress and solutions can be achieved. And they will be achieved.

My message today is not intended to address all the complex needs of America. I will send separate messages making specific recommendations for domestic legislation, such as General Revenue Sharing and the extension of the Voting Rights Act.

The moment has come to move in a new direction. We can do this by fashioning a new partnership between the Congress, the White House and the people we both represent.

Let us mobilize the most powerful and creative industrial nation that ever existed on this earth to put all our people to work. The emphasis of our economic efforts must now shift from inflation to jobs.

To bolster business and industry and to create new jobs, I propose a one-year tax reduction of $16 billion. Three-quarters would go to individuals and one-quarter to promote business investment. . . .

Cutting taxes, now, is essential if we are to turn the economy around. A tax cut offers the best hope of creating more jobs. Unfortunately, it will increase the size of the budget deficit. Therefore, it is more important than ever that we take steps to control the growth of Federal expenditures.

Part of our trouble is that we have been self-indulgent. For decades, we have been voting ever-increasing levels of Government benefits -- and now the bill has come due. We have been adding so many new programs that the size and growth of the Federal budget has taken on a life of its own.

One characteristic of these programs is that their cost increases automatically every year because the number of people eligible for most of these benefits increases every year. When these programs are enacted, there is no dollar amount set. No one knows what they will cost. All we know is that whatever they cost last year, they will cost more next year.

It is a question of simple arithmetic. Unless we check the excessive growth of Federal expenditures or impose on ourselves matching increases in taxes, we will continue to run huge inflationary deficits in the Federal budget. . . .

I am now in the process of preparing the budget submissions for fiscal year 1976. In that budget, I will propose legislation to restrain the growth of a number of existing programs. I have also concluded that no new spending programs can be initiated this year, except those for energy.

Further, I will not hesitate to veto any new spending programs adopted by the Congress. . . .

I submitted to the last Congress a list of budget deferrals and recisions. There will be more cuts recommended in the budget I will submit. Even so, the level of outlays for fiscal year 1976 is still much too high. Not only is it too high for this year but the decisions we make now inevitably have a major and growing impact on expenditure levels in future years. This is a fundamental issue we must jointly solve.

The economic disruption we and others are experiencing stems in part from the fact that the world price of petroleum has quadrupled in the last year. But we cannot put all of the blame on the oil-exporting nations. We in the United States are not blameless. Our growing dependence upon foreign sources has been adding to our vulnerability for years and we did nothing to prepare ourselves for an event such as the embargo of 1973.

During the 1960s, this country had a surplus capacity of crude oil, which we were able to make available to our trading partners whenever there was a disruption of supply. This surplus capacity enabled us to influence both supplies and prices of crude oil throughout the world. Our excess capacity neutralized any effort at establishing an effective cartel, and thus the rest of the world was assured of adequate supplies of oil at reasonable prices.

In the 1960s our surplus capacity vanished and, as a consequence, the latent power of the oil cartel could emergy in full force. Europe and Japan, both heavily dependent on imported oil, now struggle to keep their economies in balance. Even the United States, which is far more self-sufficient than most other industrial countries, has been put under serious pressure.

I am proposing a program which will begin to restore our country's surplus capacity in total energy. In this way, we will be able to assure ourselves reliable and adequate energy and help foster a new world energy stability for other major consuming nations. . . .

Voluntary conservation continues to be essential, but tougher programs are also needed -- and needed now. Therefore, I am using Presidential powers to raise the fee on all imported crude oil and petroleum products. Crude oil fee levels will be increased $1 per barrel on February 1, by $2 per barrel on March 1 and by $3 per barrel on April 1. I will take action to reduce undue hardship on any geographical region. The foregoing are interim administrative actions. They will be rescinded when the necessary legislation is enacted.

To that end, I am requesting the Congress to act within 90 days on a more comprehensive energy tax program. It includes:

-- Excise taxes and import fees totalling $2 per barrel on product imports and on all crude oil.

-- Deregulation of new natural gas and enactment of a natural gas excise tax.

-- Enactment of a windfall profits tax by April 1 to ensure that

oil producers do not profit unduly. At the same time
I plan to take Presidential initiative to decontrol the
price of domestic crude oil on April 1.

The sooner Congress acts, the more effective the oil conservation
program will be and the quicker the Federal revenues can be returned to
our people. . . .

Use of our most abundant domestic resource -- coal -- is severely
limited. We must strike a reasonable compromise on environmental concerns with coal. I am submitting Clean Air Act amendments which will
allow greater coal use without sacrificing our clean air goals.

I vetoed the strip mining legislation passed by the last Congress.
With appropriate changes, I will sign a revised version into law.

I am proposing a number of actions to energize our nuclear power
program. I will submit legislation to expedite nuclear licensing and the
rapid selection of sites. . . .

Increasing energy supplies is not enough. We must also take additional
steps to cut long-term consumption. I therefore propose:

-- Legislation to make thermal efficiency standards
    mandatory for all new buildings in the United States.
    These standards would be set after appropriate
    consultation with architects, builders and labor.
-- A new tax credit of up to $150 for those home
    owners who install insulation equipment.
-- The establishment of an energy conservation
    program to help low income families purchase
    insulation supplies.
-- Legislation to modify and defer automotive
    pollution standards for 5 years to enable us to
    improve new automobile gas mileage 40 percent by
    1980.

These proposals and actions, cumulatively, can reduce our dependence
on foreign energy supplies to 3-5 million barrels per day by 1985. To
make the United States invulnerable to foreign disruption, I propose standby emergency legislation and a strategic storage program of 1 billion barrels for defense purposes. . . .

From adversity, let us seize opportunity. Revenues of some $30 bil-
lion from higher energy taxes designed to encourage conservation must
be refunded to the American people in a manner which corrects distortions
in our tax system wrought by inflation.

People have been pushed into higher tax brackets by inflation with a
consequent reduction in their actual spending power. Business taxes are
similarly distorted because inflation exaggerates reported profits re-
sulting in excessive taxes.

Accordingly, I propose that future individual income taxes be reduced
by $16.5 billion. This will be done by raising the low income allowance
and reducing tax rates. This continuing tax cut will primarily benefit

lower and middle income taxpayers. . . .

State and local governments will receive $2 billion in additional reve-
nue sharing to offset their increased energy costs.

To offset inflationary distortions and to generate more economic activity, the corporate tax rate will be reduced from 48 percent to 42 percent.

Now, let me turn to the international dimension of the present crisis.
At no time in our peacetime history has the state of the Nation depended
more heavily on the state of the world. And seldom if ever has the state
of the world depended more heavily on the state of our Nation.

The economic distress is global. We will not solve it at home unless
we help to remedy the profound economic dislocation abroad. World trade
and monetary structure provides markets, energy, food and vital raw
materials -- for all nations. This international system is now in jeopardy.

This Nation can be proud of significant achievements in recent years
in solving problems and crises. The Berlin Agreement, the SALT agreements, our new relationship with Chica, the unprecedented efforts in the
Middle East -- are immensely encouraging. But the world is not free
from crisis. In a world of 150 nations, where nuclear technology is pro-
liferating and regional conflicts continue, international security cannot be
taken for granted.

So let there be no mistake about it: international cooperation is a
vital fact of our lives today. This is not a moment for the American people to turn inward. More than ever before, our own well-being depends
on America's determination and leadership in the world. . . .

A resurgent American economy would do more to restore the confidence of the world in its own future than anything else we can do. The
program that this Congress will pass can demonstrate to the world that we
have started to put our own house in order. It can show that this Nation is
able and willing to help other nations meet the common challenge. It can
demonstrate that the United States will fulfill its responsibility as a leader
among nations.

At stake is the future of the industrialized democracies, which have
perceived their destiny in common and sustained it in common for 30
years.

The developing nations are also at a turning point. The poorest nations see their hopes of feeding their hungry and developing their societies
shattered by the economic crisis. The long-term economic future for the
producers of raw materials also depends on cooperative solutions.

Our relations with the Communist countries are a basic factor of the
world environment. We must seek to build a long-term basis for coexis-
tence. We will stand by our principles and our interests; we will act firmly
when challenged. The kind of world we want depends on a broad policy of
creating mutual incentives for restraint and for cooperation.

As we move forward to meet our global challenges and opportunities,
we must have the tools to do the job.

Our military forces are strong and ready. This military strength deters aggression against our allies, stabilizes our relations with former adversaries and protects our homeland. Fully adequate conventional and strategic forces cost many billions, but these dollars are sound insurance for our safety and a more peaceful world.

Military strength alone is not sufficient. Effective diplomacy is also essential in preventing conflict and building world understanding. The Vladivostok negotiations with the Soviet Union represent a major step in moderating strategic arms competition. My recent discussions with leaders of the Atlantic Community, Japan and South Korea have contributed to our meeting the common challenge.

But we have serious problems before us that require cooperation between the President and the Congress. By the Constitution and tradition, the execution of foreign policy is the responsibility of the President.

In recent years, under the stress of the Vietnam War, legislative restrictions on the President's capability to execute foreign and military decisions have proliferated. As a member of the Congress, I opposed some and approved others. As President, I welcome the advice and cooperation of the House and Senate.

But, if our foreign policy is to be successful we cannot rigidly restrict in legislation the ability of the President to act. The conduct of negotiations is ill suited to such limitations. For my part, I pledge this Administration will act in the closest consultations with the Congress as we face delicate situations and troubled times throughout the globe.

When I became President only five months ago, I promised the last Congress a policy of communication, conciliation, compromise and cooperation. I renew that pledge to the new members of this Congress.

To sum up:

America needs a new direction which I have sought to chart here today -- a change of course which will:

   -- put the unemployed back to work;

   -- increase real income and production;

   -- restrain the growth of government spending;

   -- achieve energy independence; and

   -- advance the cause of world understanding

We have the ability. We have the know-how. In partnership with the American people, we will achieve these objectives.

As our 200th anniversary approaches, we owe it to ourselves, and to posterity, to rebuild our political and economic strength. Let us make America, once again, and for centuries more to come, what it has so long been -- a stronghold and beacon-light of liberty for the world.

ADDRESS TO THE CONGRESS ON SOUTHEAST ASIA
APRIL 10, 1975

Future historians will undoubtedly cite with
approval the decency and humility that Ford
displayed in the White House. Equally certain is the emphasis they will place upon his
fiscal conservation and his belief in a strong
military establishment. His tax cut and
energy proposals were radically altered by a
Democratic Congress and ushered in a period
of confrontation. On March 29, for example,
the President reluctantly signed a $23 billion
tax cut which he thought unwise. That day
amply illustrated the complexities of the presidency, however, for not only did Ford have to
accept a bill he disliked but also, half a world
away, the city of Danang fell to the North Vietnamese Army. That unfolding tragedy wrenched
the eyes of the nation away from domestic
politics and for the next month Ford desperately
tried to salvage some honor from the shambles
of our Vietmanese experience. He summarized
his position in a major speech to the Congress.

Source: White House Press Release,
April 10, 1975.

I stand before you tonight after many agonizing hours in very solemn
prayers for guidance by the Almighty. In my report on the State of the
Union in January, I concentrated on two subjects, which were uppermost
in the minds of the American people -- urgent actions for the recovery
of our economy, and a comprehensive program to make the United States
independent of foreign sources of energy.
    I thank the Congress for the action that it has taken thus far in my re-
sponse for economic recommendations. I look forward to early approval
of a national energy program to meet our country's long-range and emergency needs in the field of energy.
    Tonight it is my purpose to review our relations with the rest of the
world in the spirit of candor and consultation, which I have sought to
maintain with my former colleagues and with our countrymen from the
time that I took office.
    It is the first priority of my Presidency to sustain and strengthen the
mutual trust and respect which must exist among Americans and their
government if we are to deal successfully with the challenges confronting

us both at home and abroad.

The leadership of the United States of America since the end of World War II has sustained and advanced the security, well being and freedom of millions of human beings besides ourselves . . . .

Tonight is a time for straight talk among friends, about where we stand and where we are going.

A vast human tragedy has befallen our friends in Vietnam and Cambodia. Tonight I shall not talk only about obligations arising from legal documents. Who can forget the enormous sacrifices of blood, dedication and treasure that we made in Vietnam?

Under five Presidents and 12 Congresses, the United States was engaged in Indochina. Millions of Americans served, thousands died, and many more were wounded, imprisoned or lost.

Over $150 billion have been appropriated for that war by the Congress of the United States. And after years of effort, we negotiated under the most difficult circumstances a settlement, which made it possible for us to remove our military forces and bring home with pride our American prisoners.

This settlement, if its terms had been adhered to, would have permitted our South Vietnamese ally, with our material and moral support, to maintain its security and rebuild after two decades of war.

The chances for an enduring peace after the last American fighting man left Vietnam in 1973, rested on two publicly states premises. First, that if necessary, the United States would help sustain the terms of the Paris accords it signed two years ago. Second, that the United States would provide adequate economic and military assistance to South Vietnam.

Let us refresh our memories for just a moment. The universal consensus in the United States, at that time, late 1972, was that if we could end our own involvement and obtain the release of our prisoners, we would provide adequate material support to South Vietnam.

The North Vietnamese, from the moment they signed the Paris accords, systematically violated the case-fire and other provisions of that agreement. Flagrantly disregarding the ban on the infiltration of troops, the North Vietnamese illegally introduced over 350,000 men into the South. In direct violation of the agreement, they sent in the most modern equipment in massive amounts. Meanwhile, they continued to receive large quantities of supplies and arms from their friends.

In the face of this situation, the United States -- torn as it was by the emotions of a decade of war -- was unable to respond. We deprived ourselves by law of the ability to enforce the agreement thus giving North Vietnam assurance that it could violate that agreement with impunity.

Next, we reduced our economic and arms aid to South Vietnam. Finally, we signaled our increasing reluctance to give any support to that nation struggling for its survival.

Encouraged by these developments, the North Vietnamese, in recent months, began sending even their reserve divisions into South Vietnam.

Some 20 divisions, virtually their entire army, are now in South Vietnam.

The government of South Vietnam, uncertain of further American assistance, hastily ordered a strategic withdrawal to more defensible positions. The extremely difficult maneuver, decided upon without consultations, was poorly executed, hampered by floods of refugees and thus led to panic. The results are painfully obvious and profoundly moving. . . .

With respect to North Vietnam, I call upon Hanoi, and ask the Congress to join with me in this call, to cease military operations immediately and to honor the terms of the Paris agreement.

The United States is urgently requesting the signatories of the Paris Conference to meet their obligations to use their influence to halt the fighting and to enforce the 1973 accords.

Diplomatic notes to this effect have been sent to all members of the Paris Conference, including the Soviet Union and the People's Republic of China.

The situation in South Vietnam and Cambodia has reached a critical phase requiring immediate and positive decisions by this government. The options before us are few and the time is very short.

On the one hand, the United States could do nothing more. Let the government of South Vietnam save itself and what is left of its territory, if it can. Let those South Vietnamese civilians who have worked with us for a decade or more save their lives and their families, if they can.

In short, shut our eyes and wash our hands of the whole affair, if we can.

Or, on the other hand, I could ask the Congress for authority to enforce the Paris accords with our troops and our tanks and our aircraft and our artillery, and carry the war to the enemy.

There are two narrow options: First, stick with my January request that Congress appropriate $300 million for military assistance for South Vietnam and seek additional funds for economic and humanitarian purposes, or increase my request for both emergency military and humanitarian assistance to levels which, by best estimates, might enable the South Vietnamese to stem the onrushing aggression, to stabilize the military situation, permit the chance of a negotiated political settlement between the North and South Vietnamese and, if the very worst were to happen, at least allow the orderly evacuation of Americans and endangered South Vietnamese to places of safety.

Let me now state my considerations and my conclusions.

I have received a full report from General Weyand, who I sent to Vietnam to assess the situation. He advises that the current military situation is very critical, but that South Vietnam is continuing to defend itself with the resources available.

However, he feels that if there is to be any chance of success for their defense plan, South Vietnam needs urgently an additional $722 million in very specific military supplies from the United States.

In my judgment, a stabilization of the military situation offers the best opportunity for a political solution. . . .

I am also mindful of our posture toward the rest of the world, and particularly of our future relations with the free nations of Asia. These nations must not think for a minute that the United States is pulling out on them or intends to abandon them to agression.

I have, therefore, concluded that the national interests of the United States and the cause of world stability require that we continue to give both military and humanitarian assistance to the South Vietnamese.

Assistance to South Vietnam at this stage must be swift and adequate. Drift and indecision invite far deeper disaster. The sums I had requested before the major North Vietnamese offensive and the sudden South Vietnamese retreat are obviously inadequate.

Half-hearted action would be worse than none. We must act together and act decicisively.

I am, therefore, asking the Congress to appropriate without delay $722 million for emergency military assistance, and an initial sum of $250 million for economic and humanitarian aid for South Vietnam.

The situation in South Vietnam is changing very rapidly, and the need for emergency food, medicine and refugee relief is growing by the hour. I will work with the Congress in the days ahead to develop humanitarian assistance to meet these very pressing needs.

Fundamental decency requires that we do everything in our power to ease the misery and the pain of the monumental human crisis which has befallen the people of Vietnam. Millions have fled in the face of the Communist onslaught and are now homeless and are now destitute.

I hereby pledge in the name of the American people that the United States will make a maximum humanitarian effort to help care for and feed these hopeless victims.

Now I ask the Congress to clarify immediately its restrictions on the use of U.S. military forces in Southeast Asia for the limited purposes of protecting American lives by ensuring their evacuation, if this should be necessary.

I also ask prompt revision of the law to cover those Vietnamese to whom we have a very special obligation and whose lives may be endangered should the worst come to pass. . . .

Members of the Congress, my fellow Americans, this moment of tragedy for Indochina is a time of trial for us. It is a time for national resolve.

It has been said that the United States is over-extended, that we have too many commitments too far from home, that we must re-examine what our truly vital interests are and shape our strategy to conform to them.

I find no fault with this as a theory, but in the real world, such a course must be pursued carefully and in close coordination with solid progress toward overall reduction in worldwide tensions.

We cannot, in the meantime, abandon our friends while our adversaries support and encourage theirs. We cannot dismantle our defenses, our diplomacy or our intelligence capability while other increase and strengthen theirs.

Let us put an end to self-inflicted wounds. Let us remember that our national unity is a most priceless asset. Let us deny our adversaries the satisfaction of using Vietnam to pit Americans against Americans.

At this moment, the United States must present to the world a united front. Above all, let's keep events in Southeast Asia in their proper perspective. The security and the progress of hundreds of millions of people everywhere depend importantly on us.

Let no potential adversary believe that our difficulties or our debates mean a slackening of our national will. We will stand by our friends, we will honor our commitments, and we will uphold our country's principles.

The American people know that our strength, our authority and our leadership have helped prevent a third world war for more than a generation. We will not shrink from this duty in the decades ahead.

ADDRESS TO THE NATION ON ENERGY POLICY
MAY 27, 1975

Congress ignored Ford's urgent call for more
aid; Vietnam and Cambodia collapsed in living
color on the TV screens of America.
National energy policy illustrated the deadlock between the executive and legislative branches
during 1975. Questions of increased production,
higher prices, crude oil imports, reserve levels,
gasoline conservation, marginal wells and deple-
tion allowances were debated ad nauseum; yet
nothing was done. Ford summarized his views
and acted to implement his beliefs in May.

Source: White House Press Release,
May 27, 1975.

Last January 15, I went before your Senators and Representatives in
Congress with a comprehensive plan to make our country independent of
foreign sources of energy by 1985. Such a program was long overdue.
We have become increasingly at the mercy of others for the fuel on which
our entire economy runs.

Here are the facts and figures that will not go away. The United
States is dependent on foreign sources for about 37 percent of its present
petroleum needs. In ten years, if we do nothing, we will be importing
more than half of our oil at prices fixed by others, if they choose to sell
to us at all.

In two and a half years, we will be twice as vulnerable to a foreign
oil embargo as we were two winters ago. We are now paying out $25 bil-
lion a year for foreign oil. Five years ago we paid out only $3 billion
annually. Five years from now, if we do nothing, who knows how many
more billions will be flowing out of the United States.

These are not just American dollars. These are American jobs.

Four months ago, I sent the Congress this 167-page draft of detailed
legislation, plus some additional tax proposals. My program was designed
to conserve the energy we now have, while at the same time speeding up
the development and production of new domestic energy.

Although this would increase the cost of energy until new supplies
were fully tapped, those dollars would remain in this country and would
be returned to our own economy through tax cuts and rebates. I asked the
Congress in January to enact this urgent ten-year program for energy
independence within 80 days; that is, by mid-April.

In the meantime, to get things going, I said I would use the standby
Presidential authority granted by the Congress to reduce our use of foreign
petroleum by raising import fees on each barrel of crude oil by $1.00 on
February 1, another $1.00 on March 1, and a third on April 1.

As soon as Congress acted on my comprehensive energy program, I promised to take off these inport fees. I imposed the first dollar on oil imports February 1, making appropriate exemptions for hardship situations.

Now, what did the Congress do in February about energy? Congress did nothing.

Nothing, that is, except rush through legislation suspending for 90 days my authority to impose any import fees on foreign oil. Congress needed time, they said.

At the end of February, the Democratic leaders of the House and Senate and other Members concerned with energy came to the White House. They gave me this pamphlet outlining energy goals similar to mine and promised to come up with a Congressional energy program better than men mine by the end of April.

I remember one of them saying he didn't see how they could ask the President to do more than postpone the second dollar for 60 days. If the Congress couldn't come up with an energy program by then, he said, go ahead and put it on.

Their request stretched my original deadline by a couple of weeks. But I wanted to be reasonable, I wanted to be cooperative.

So, in vetoing their bill to restrict the President's authority, I agreed to their request for a 60-day delay before taking the next step under my energy plan.

What did the Congress do in March? What did the Congress do in April about energy? Congress did nothing.

In fairness, I must say there were diligent efforts by some Members -- Democrats as well as Republicans -- to fashion meaningful energy legislation in their subcommittees and committees.

My Administration worked very hard with them to bring a real energy independence bill to a vote. At the end of April, the deadline set by the Congressional leaders themselves, I deferred for still another 30 days, the second $1.00 fee on imported oil. Even then, I still hoped for positive Congressional action.

So, what has the Congress done in May about energy? Congress did nothing and went home for a 10-day recess.

February, March, April, May, as of now, the Congress has done nothing positive to end our energy dependence.

On the contrary, it has taken two negative actions, the first an attempt to prevent the President from doing anything on his own; the second, to pass a strip mining bill which would reduce domestic coal production instead of increasing it; put thousands of people out of work; needlessly increased the cost of energy to consumers; raise electric bills for many, and compel us to import more foreign oil, not less.

I was forced to veto this anti-energy bill last week because I will not be responsible for taking one step backward on energy when the Congress will not take one step forward on energy.

The Congress has concentrated its attention on conservation measures such as a higher gasoline tax. The Congress has done little or nothing to stimulate production of new energy sources here at home.

At Elk Hills Naval Petroleum Reserve, in California, I saw oil wells waiting to produce 300,000 barrels a day if the Congress would change the law to permit it.

There are untold millions of barrels more in our Alaskan petróleum reserves and under the Continental Shelf. We could save 300,000 barrels a day if only Congress would allow more electric power plants to substitute American coal for foreign oil.

Peaceful atomic power, which we pioneered, is advancing faster abroad abroad than at home.

Still, the Congress do s nothing about energy. We are today worse off than we were in January.

Domestic oil production is going down, down, down. Natural gas production is starting to dwindle, and many areas face severe shortages next winter.

Coal production is still at levels of the 1940s. Foreign oil suppliers are considering another price increase.

I could go on and on, but you know the facts. This country needs to regain its independence from foreign sources of energy, and the sooner the better.

There is no visible energy shortage now, but we could have one overnight. We do not have an energy crisis, but we may have one next winter. We do have an energy problem, a very grave problem, but one we can still manage and solve if we are successful internationally and can act decisively domestically.

Four months are already lost. The Congress has acted only negatively. I must now do what I can do as President.

First, I will impose an additional $1.00 import fee on foreign crude oil, and 60 cents on refined products, effective June 1. I gave the Congress its 60 days, plus an extra 30 days to do something, but nothing has been done since January.

Higher fees will further discourage the consumption of imported fuel and may generate some constructive action when the Congress comes back.

Second, as I directed on April 30, the Federal Energy Administration has completed public hearings on decontrol of old domestic oil. I will submit a decontrol plan to Congress shortly after it reconvenes. Along with it, I will urge the Congress to pass a windfall profits tax with a plowback provision.

These two measures would prevent unfair gains by oil companies from decontrol prices, furnish a substantial incentive to increase domestic energy production and encourage conservation.

When I talk about energy, I am talking about jobs. Our American economy runs on energy. No energy -- no jobs.

In the longrun, it is just that simple. The sudden fourfold increase in foreign oil prices and the 1973 embargo helped to throw us into this recession. We are on our way out of this recession. Another oil embargo could throw us back.

We cannot continue to depend on the price and supply whims of others.

The Congress cannot drift, dawdle and debate forever with America's future.

I need your help to energize this Congress into comprehensive action. I will continue to press for my January program, which is still the only total energy program there is.

I cannot sit here idly while nothing is done.

ADDRESS TO THE HELSINKI CONFERENCE
AUGUST 1, 1975

The firm foundation of administration foreign
policy was the concept of detente brilliantly
pursued by Secretary of State Kissinger. To
advance his efforts toward world peace, Ford
traveled to the European Conference held in
Helsinki. On August 1, 1975, he addressed
the assembled delegates and voiced America's
hope that increased mutual respect and understanding could create a better world.

Source: <u>New York Times</u>,
August 2, 1975.

The nations assembled here have kept the general peace in Europe for
30 years. Yet there have been too many narrow escapes from major con
flict. There remains, to this day, the urgent issue of how to construct a
just and lasting peace for all peoples. I have not come across the Atlantic
to say what all of us already know: The nations now have the capacity to
destroy civilization and, therefore, all our foreign policies must have as
their one supreme objective the prevention of a thermonoclear war. Nor
have I come to dwell upon the hard realities of continuing ideological differences, political rivalries and military competition that persist among us.

I have come to Helsinki as spokesman for a nation whose vision has always been forward, whose people have always demanded that the future be
brighter than the past and whose united will and purpose at this hour is to
work diligently to promote peace and progress not only for ourselves but
for all mankind.

I am here simply to say to my colleagues:

We owe it to our children, to the children of all continents, not to miss
any opportunity, not to malinger for one minute, not to spare ourselves or
allow others to shirk in the monumental task of building a better and safer
world.

The American people, like the people of Europe, know well that mere
assertions of goodwill, passing changes in the political mood of governments,
laudable declarations of principles are not enough. But if we proceed with
care, with commitment to real progress there is now an opportunity to turn
our peoples' hopes into realities.

In recent years nations represented here have sought to ease potential
conflicts. But much more remains to be done before we prematurely congratulate ourselves.

Military competition must be controlled.

Political competition must be restrained.

Crises must not be manipulated or exploited for unilateral advantages
that could lead us again to the brink of war.

The process of negotiation must be sustained, not at a snail's pace,
but with demonstrated enthusiasm and visible progress....

This conference is part of that process -- a challenge, not a conclusion. We face unresolved problems of military security in Europe. We
face them with very real differences in values and aims. But if we deal with
them with careful preparation, if we focus on concrete issues and if we
maintain forward movement, we have the right to expect real progress.

The era of confrontation that has divided Europe since the end of the
Second World War may now be ending. There is a new perception and a
shared perception of a change for the better, away from confrontation and
toward new possibilities for secure and mutually beneficial cooperation.
That is what we all have been saying here. I welcome and I share these
hopes for the future.

The postwar policy of the United States has been consistently directed
toward the rebuilding of Europe and the rebirth of Europe's historic iden-
tity. The nations of the West have worked together for peace and progress
throughout Europe. From the start we have taken the initiative by stating
clear goals and areas for negotiation.

We have sought a structure of European relations, tempering rivalry
with restraint, power with moderation building upon the traditional bonds
that link us with old friends and reaching out to forge new ties with former
and potential adversaries.

In recent years there have been some substantial achievements.

We see the four-power agreement on Berlin of 1971 as the end of a pe-
rennial crisis that on at least three occasions brought the world to the
brink of doom.

The agreements between the Federal Republic of Germany and the
states of Eastern Europe, and the related intra-German accords, enable
Central Europe and the world to breathe easier.

The start of East-West talks on mutual and balanced force reductions
demonstrated determination to deal with military-security problems on the
Continent.

The 1972 treaty between the United States and the Soviet Union to limit
antiballistic missiles, and the interim agreement limiting strategic offensive weapons, were the first solid break-throughs in what must be a continuing, long-term process of limiting strategic nuclear arsenals.

I profoundly hope that this conference will spur further practical and
concrete results. It affords a welcome opportunity to widen the circle of
those countries involved in easing tensions between East and West. Participation in the work of detente and participation in the benefits of detente
must be everybody's business -- in Europe and elsewhere. But detente can
succeed only if everybody understands what detente actually is.

First, detente is an evolutionary process, not a static condition. Many
formidable challenges yet remain.

Second, the success of the detente process depends on new behavior patterns that give life to all our solemn declarations. The goals we are stating today are the yardstick by which our performance will be measured.

The people of all Europe and, I assure you, the people of North America are thoroughly tired of having their hopes raised and then shattered by empty words and unfulfilled pledges. We had better say what we mean and mean what we say, or we will have the anger of our citizens to answer.

While we must not expect miracles, we can and do expect steady progress that comes in steps -- steps that are related to each other and that link our actions with our words in various areas of our relations.

Finally, there must be an acceptance of mutual obligation. Detente, as I have often said, must be a two-way street. Tensions cannot be eased by one side alone. Both sides must want detente and work to achieve it. Both sides must benefit from it....

These documents which we will sign represent another step -- how long or short a step only time will tell -- in the process of detente and reconciliation in Europe. Our people will be watching and measuring our progress. They will ask how these noble sentiments are being translated into actions that bring about a more secure and just order in the daily lives of each of our nations and its citizens.

The documents produced here represent compromises like all international negotiations -- but these principles we have agreed upon are more than the lowest common denominator of governmental positions.

They affirm the most fundamental human rights: liberty of thought, conscience and faiths; the exercise of civil and political rights; the rights of minorities.

They call for a freer flow of information, ideas and people: greater scope for the press, cultural and educational exchange, family reunification, the right to travel and to marriage between nationals of different states, and for the protection of the priceless heritage of our diverse cultures.

They offer wide areas for greater cooperation: trade, industrial production, science and technology, the environment, transportation, health, space and the oceans.

They reaffirm the basic principles of relations between states: nonintervention, sovereign equality, self determination, territorial integrity, inviolability of frontiers and the possibility of change by peaceful means.

The United States gladly subscribes to this document because we subscribe to every one of these principles. . . .

To our fellow participants in this conference my presence here symbolizes my country's bital interest in Europe's future. Our future is bound with yours. Our economic well-being as well as our security is linked increasingly with common destiny. The United States therefore intends to participate fully in the affairs of Europe and in truning the results of this conference into a living reality.

To America's allies: We in the West must pursue the course upon

which we have embarked together, reinforced by one another's strength
and mutual confidence. Stability in Europe requires equilibrium in Europe,
therefore I assure you that my country will continue to be a concerned and
reliable partner. Our partnership is far more than a matter of formal
agreements. It is a reflection of beliefs, traditions and ties that are of
deep significance to the American people. We are proud that these values
are expressed in this document.

To the countries of the East:

The United States considers that the principles on which this conference
has agreed are part of the great heritage of European civilization which we
all hold in trust for all mankind. To my country, they are not cliches or
empty phrases. We take this work and these words seriously. We will
spare no effort to ease tensions and solve problems between us. But it is
important that you recognize the deep devotion of the American people and
their Government to human rights and fundamental freedoms and thus to
the pledges that this conference has made regarding the freer movement of
people, ideas and information. . . .

Military stability in Europe has kept the peace. While maintaining that
stability, it is now time to reduce substantially the high levels of military
forces on both sides. Negotiations now under way in Vienna on mutual and
balanced force reductions so far have not produced the results for which I
had hoped. The United States stands ready to demonstrate flexibility in
moving these negotiations forward if others will do the same. An agreement that enhances mutual security is feasible -- and essential.

The United States also intends to pursue vigorously a further agreement
on strategic arms limitation with the Soviet Union. This remains a priority of American policy.

General Secretary Brezhnev and I agreed last November in Vladivostok
on the essentials of a new accord limiting strategic offensive weapons for
the next 10 years. We are moving forward in our bilateral discussions here
in Helsinki. . . .

Our people want a better future. Their expectations have been raised
by the very real steps that have already been taken -- in arms control, political negotiations and expansion of contacts and economic relations. Our
presence here offers them further hope. We must not let them down.

If the Soviet Union and the United States can reach agreement so that
our astronauts can fit together the most intricate scientific equipment, work
together and shake hands 137 miles out in space, we as statesmen have an
obligation to do as well on earth.

History will judge this conference not by what we say today, but what
we do tomorrow -- not by the promises we make but by the promises we
keep.

FORD DEALS WITH NEW YORK

Despite the debates over taxes, energy policy
and detente, perhaps the most emotional issue of 1975 was the prospective bankruptcy
of the city of New York. Poor leadership and
inept financial management had driven that
city to the brink of default. Federal aid
seemed its last hope. Yet Ford, advised
closely by Secretary Simon and Vice President
Rockefeller, was convinced that the city was
not deserving of any help. Only when he came
to understand the catastrophic effects a New
York bankruptcy would generate did the president reverse policy and approve a seasonal
loan program. The city never forgave Ford's
callousness and cast a huge vote against him
in 1976.

Source: New York Times,
October 30, November 27, 1975.

I am deeply grateful for the opportunity to join you today and talk to
you about a matter of very deep concern to all Americans.

New York City, where one out of every 25 Americans lives, through
whose Golden Door untold million have entered this land of liberty, faces a
financial showdown.

The time has come for straight talk -- to these eight million Americans
and to the other 206 million Americans to whom I owe the duty of stating my
convictions and my conclusions, and to you, whose job it is to carry them
throughout the world as well as the United States.

The time has come to sort facts and figures from fiction and fear-mon-
gering in this terribly complex situation. The time has come to say what
solutions will work and which should be cast aside.

And the time has come for all Americans to consider how the problems
of New York and the hard decisions they demand foreshadow and focus upon
potential problems for all government -- Federal, state and local -- problems which demand equally hard decisions for them.

One week ago New York City tottered on the brink of financial default
which was deferred only at the eleventh hour.

The next day Mayor Beame testified here in Washington that the financial resources of the city and the state of New York were exhausted. Governor Carey agreed.

They said, it's now up to Washington. And unless the Federal Govern-

ment intervenes, New York City within a short time will no longer be able
to pay its bills.

The message was clear: responsibility for New York City's financial
problems is being left on the front doorstep of the Federal Government --
unwanted and abandoned by its real parents.

Many explanations have been offered about what led New York City
deeper and deeper into this quagmire.

Some contend it was long-range economic factors such as the flight to
the suburbs of the city's more affluent citizens, the migration to the city
of poorer people, and the departure of industry.

Others argued that the big metropolitan city has become obsolescent,
that decay and pollution have brought a deterioration in the quality of
urban life, and New York's downfall could not be prevented.

Let's face one simple fact: most other cities in America have faced
these very same challenges, and they are still financially healthy today.
They have not been luckier than New York; they simply have been better
managed.

There is an old saying: "The harder you try, the luckier you get."
And I kind of like that definition of "luck."

During the last decade, the officials of New York City have allowed
its budget to triple. No city can expect to remain solvent if it allows its
expenses to increase by an average of 12 per cent every year, while its tax
revenues are increasing by only 4 to 5 per cent per year.

As Al Smith, a great Governor of New York who came from the side-
walks of New York City, used to say: "Let's look at the record."

The record shows that New York City's wages and salaries are the
highest in the United States. A sanitation worker with three years' experience now receives a base salary of nearly $15,000 a year. Fringe benefits
and retirement costs average more than 50 per cent of base pay. There
are four-week paid vacations and unlimited sick leave after only one year
on the job.

The record shows that in most cities, municipal employees have to
pay 50 per cent or more of the cost of their pensions. New York City is
the only major city in the country that picks up the entire burden.

The record shows that when New York's municipal employes retire
they often retire much earlier than in most cities and at pensions consider-
ably higher than sound retirement plans permit.

The record shows New York City has 18 municipal hospitals; yet on
an average day, 25 per cent of the hospital beds are empty. Meanwhile,
the city spends millions more to pay the hospital expenses of those who use
private hospitals.

The record shows New York City operates one of the largest univer-
sities in the world, free of tuition for any high school graduate, rich or
poor, who wants to attend.

As for New York's much-discussed welfare burden, the record shows
more than one current welfare recipient in 10 may be legally ineligible for

welfare assistance.

Certainly I do not blame all the good people of New York City for their generous instincts or for their present plight. I do blame those who have misled the people of New York about the inevitable consequences of what they are doing or were doing over the last 10 years.

The consequences have been:

A steady stream of unbalanced budgets.

Massive growth in the city's debt.

Extraordinary increases in public employee contracts.

And total disregard of independent experts who warned again and again that the city was courting disaster.

There can be no doubt where the real responsibility lies. And when New York City now asks the rest of the country to guarantee its bills, it can be no surprise that many other American ask why.

Why, they ask, should they support advantages in New York that they have not been able to afford for their own communities?

Why, they ask, should all the working people of this country be forced to rescue those who bankrolled New York City's policies for so long -- the large investors and big banks?

In my judgment, no one has yet given these questions a satisfactory answer.

Instead, Americans are being told that unless the rest of the country bails out New York, there will be catastrophe for the United States and perhaps for the world.

Is this scare story true?

Of course there are risks that default could cause temporary fluctuations in the financial markets. But these markets have already made a substantial adjustment in anticipation of a possible default by New York City.

Claims are made that because of New York City's troubles, other municipalities will have grave difficulty selling their bonds. I know that this troubles many thoughtful citizens.

But, the New York City record of bad financial management is unique among municipalities throughout the United States. Other communities have a solid reputation for living within their means. In recent days and weeks, other local governments have gone to investors with clean records of fiscal responsibility and have had no difficulty raising funds.

The greater risk is that any attempt to provide a Federal blank check for the leaders of New York City would insure that no long-run solution to the city's problems will ever occur.

I can understand the concern of many citizens in New York and elsewhere. I understand because I'm also concerned.

What I cannot understand -- and what nobody should condone is the blatant attempt in some quarters to frighten the American people and their representatives in Congress into panicky support of patently bad policy. The people of this country will not be stampeded; they will not panic when

a few desperate New York officials and bankers try to scare New York's
mortgage payments out of them.

We've heard enough scare talk.

What we need now is a calm, rational decision as to what is the right
solution -- the solution that is best for the people of New York and best for
all Americans.

To be effective, the right solution must meet three basic tests:

It must maintain essential public services for the people of New York
City. It must protect the innocent victims of this tragedy. There must
be policemen on the beat, firemen in the station, nurses in the emergency
wards.

Second, the solution must assure that New York City can and will achieve and maintain a balanced budget in the years ahead.

And third, the right solution must guarantee that neither New York
City nor any other American city ever becomes a ward of the Federal Government. . . .

What is the solution to New York's dilemma?

There are at least eight different proposals under consideration by the
Congress intended to prevent default. They are all variations of one basic
theme: that the Federal Government should, or would, guarantee the avail-
ability of funds to New York City.

I can tell you -- and tell you now -- that I am prepared to veto any
bill that has as its purpose a Federal bailout of New York City to prevent
default.

I am fundamentally opposed to this so-called solution, and I'll tell you
why.

Basically, it's a mirage. By giving a Federal guarantee we would be
reducing rather than increasing the prospect that the city's budget will
ever be balanced. New York City's officials have proved in the past that
they will not face up to the city's massive network of pressure groups as
long as any other alternative is available. If they can scare the whole country into providing that alternative now, why shouldn1t they be confident they
can scare us again into providing it three years from now? In short, it encourages the continuation of "politics as usual" in New York -- which is
precisely not the way to solve the problem.

Such a step would set a terrible precedent for the rest of the nation.
It would promise immediate rewards and eventual rescue to every other
city that follows the tragic example of our largest city. What restraint
would be left on the spending of other local and state governments once it
becomes clear that there is a Federal rescue squad that will always arrive
in the nick of time?

Finally, we must all recognize who the primary beneficiaries of a
Federal guarantee program would be. The beneficiaries would not be
those who live and work in New York City because the really essential
public services must and will continue.

The primary beneficiary would be the New York official who would es-

cape responsibility for their past folly and be further excused from making
the hard decisions required now to restore the city's fiscal integrity.

The secondary beneficiary would be the large investors and financial
institutions who purchased these securities anticipating a high rate of tax-
free return.

Does this mean there is no solution? Not at all. There is a fair and
sensible way to resolve this issue, and this is the way to do it.

If the city is unable to act to provide a means of meeting its obligations,
a new law is required to assure an orderly and fair mean of handling the
situation.

As you know, the Constitution empowers the Congress to enact uniform
bankruptcy laws. Therefore, I will submit to the Congress special legislation providing the Federal courts with sufficient authority to preside over
an orderly reorganization of New York City's financial affairs -- should
that become necessary.

How would this work? The city, with state approval, would file a petition with the Federal District Court in New York under a proposed new
Chapter XVI of the Bankruptcy Act. The petition would state that New York
is unable to pay its debts as they mature and would be accompanied by a
proposed way to work out an adjustment of its debts with its creditior.

The Federal Court would then be authorized to accept jurisdiction of the
the case. There would be an automatic stay of suits by creditors so that
the essential functions of the city would not be disrupted.

It would provide a breathing space for an orderly plan to be developed
so that the city could work out arrangements with its creditors.

While New York City works out a compromise with its creditors the
essential governmental functions of the city would continue.

In the event of default, the Federal Government will work with the court
to assure that police and fire and other essential services for the protection
of life and property in New York are maintained.

The proposed legislation will include provision that as a condition of
New York City petitioning the court, the city must not only file a good faith
plan for payments to its creditors but must also present a program for
placing the fiscal affairs of the city on a sound basis.

In order to meet the short-term needs of New York City the court
would be empowered to authorize debt certificates future revenues ahead
of other creditors.

Thus, the legislation I am proposing will do three essential things.

First, it will prevent, in the event of default, all New York City funds
from being tied up in lawsuits.

Second, it will provide the conditions for an orderly plan to be developed
for payments to New York City's creditors over the long term.

Third, it will provide a way for new borrowing to be secured by pledging future revenues.

I don't want anybody misled. This proposed legislation will not, by
itself, put the affairs of New York City in order. Some hard measures

must be taken by the officials of New York City and New York State. They must either increase revenues or cut expenditures or devise some combination that will bring them to a sound financial position. Careful examination has convinced me that those measures are not beyond the demands of reason, neither beyond the realm of possibility nor beyond the demands of reason. If they are taken, New York City will, with the assistance of the legislation I am proposing, be able to restore itself as a fully solvent operation.

To summarize, the approach I am recommending is this: If New York fails to act in its own behalf, orderly proceedings would then be supervised by a Federal court.

The ones who would be most affected by this course of action would be those who are now fighting, tooth and nail to protect their authority and to protect their investments: New York City's officials and the city's creditors. The creditors will not be wiped out; how much they will be hurt will depend upon the future conduct of the city's leaders.

For the people of New York, this plan will mean that essential services will continue. There may be some temporary inconveniences, but that will be true of any solution that is adopted.

For the financial community, the default may bring some temporary difficulties but the repercussions should not be large or long-standing.

Finally, for the people of the United States, this means that they will not be asked to assume a burden that is not of their own making and should not become their responsibility. This is a fair and sensible way to proceed.

There is a profound lesson for all Americans in the financial experience of our biggest and our richest city.

Though we are the richest nation, the richest nation in the world, there is a practical limit to our public bounty, just as there is to New York City's.

Other cities, other states as well as the Federal Government are not immune to the insidious desease from which New York is suffering. This sickness is brought on by years and years of higher spending, higher deficits, more inflation and more borrowing to pay for higher spending, higher deficits and so on and so on and so on. It's a progressive disease and there is no painless cure.

Those who have been treating New York's financial sickness have been prescribing larger and larger doses of the same political stimulants that has proved so popular and successful in Washington for so many years.

None of us can point a completely guiltless finger at New York City. None of us should now derive comfort or pleasure from New York's anguish. But neither can we let that contagion spread.

As we work with the wonderful people of New York to overcome their difficulties -- and they will -- we must never forget what brought this great center of human civilization to the brink.

If we go on spending more than we have, providing more benefits and more services than we can pay for, then a day of reckoning will come to Washington and the whole country just as is has to New York City.

And so, let me conclude with one question of my own:

When that day of reckoning comes, who will bail out the United States of America?. . .

*   *   *   *   *   *   *

I would like to comment briefly on recent developments in New York.

Since early this year, and particularly in the last few weeks, the leaders of New York State and of New York City have been working to overcome the financial difficulties of the city, which as the result of many years of unsound fiscal practices, unbalanced budgets and increased borrowing threatening to bring about municipal bankruptcy of an unprecedented magnitude.

As you know, I have been steadfastly opposed to any Federal help for New York City which would permit them to avoid responsibility for managing their own affairs. I will not allow the taxpayers of other states and cities to pay the price of New York's past political errors. It is important to all of us that the fiscal integrity of New York City be restored and that the personal security of eight million Americans in New York City be fully assured.

It has always been my hope that the leaders of New York, when the chips were down, face up to their responsibilities and take the tough decisions that the facts of the situation require. That is still my hope. And I must say that it is much, much closer to reality today than it was last spring. I have quite frankly been surprised that they have come as far as they have. I doubted that they would act unless ordered to do so by a Federal court.

Only in the last month, after I made it clear that New York would have to solve its fundamental financial problems without the help of the Federal taxpayer, has there been a concerted effort to put the finances of the city and the state on a sound basis. They have today informed me of the specifics of New York's self-help program. This includes:

This includes meaningful spending cuts have been approved to reduce the cost of running the city. Two, more than $200 million in new taxes have been voted. Three, payment to the city's noteholders will be postponed and interest payments will be reduced through the passage of legislation by New York State. Four, banks and other large institutions have agreed to wait to collect on their loans and to accept lower interest rates. Five, for the first time in years members of municipal unions will be required to bear part of the cost of pension contributions and other reforms will be made in union pension plans. Six, the city pension system is to provide additional loans up to $2.5 billion to the city. All of these steps -- adding up to $4 billion -- are part of an effort to provide financing and to bring the city's budget into balance by the fiscal year beginning July 1, 1977.

Only a few months ago, we were told that all of these reforms were impossible and could not be accomplished by New York alone. Today they are being done.

This is a realistic program. I want to commend all of those involved in New York City and New York State for their constructive efforts to date.

I have been closely watching their progress in meeting their problem. However, in the next few months New York will lack enough funds to cover its day-to-day operating expenses.

This problem is caused by the city having to pay its bills on a daily basis throughout the year; while the bulk of its revenues are received during spring. Most cities are able to borrow short-term funds to cover these needs, traditionally repaying them within their fiscal year.

Because the private credit market may remain closed to them representatives of New York have informed me and my Administration that they have acted in good faith, but they still need to borrow money on a short-term basis for a period of time each of the next two years in order to provide essential services to the eight million Americans who live in the nation's largest city.

Therefore, I have decided to ask the Congress when it returns from recess for authority to provide a temporary line of credit to the State of New York to enable it to supply seasonal financing of essential services for the people of New York City.

There will be stringent conditions.

Funds would be loaned to the state on a seasonal basis normally from July through March to be repaid with interest in April, May and June when the bulk of the city's revenues comes in.

All Federal loans will be repaid in full at the end of each year. There will be no cost to the rest of the taxpayers of the United States.

This is only the beginning of New York's recovery process, and not the end. New York officials must continue to accept primary responsibility. There must be no misunderstanding of my position. If local parties fail to carry out their plan, I am prepared to stop even the seasonal Federal a assistance. I again ask the Congress promptly to amend the Federal bankruptcy laws so that if the New York plan fails, there will be an orderly procedure available.

A fundamental issue is involved here; sound fiscal management is imperative of self-government. I trust we have all learned the hard lesson that no individual, no family, no business, no city, no state and no nation, can go on indefinitely spending more money than it takes in.

As we count our Thanksgiving blessings, we recall that Americans have always believed in helping those who help themselves. New York has finally taken the tough decision it had to take to help itself. In making the required sacrifices, the people of New York have earned the encouragement of the rest of the country.

THE STATE OF THE UNION
JANUARY 20, 1976

The year 1976 celebrated the bicentennial of
our nation and represented a time of choice
for the American people. Ford's political
beliefs had been well established - fiscal
prudence, military sufficiency, a distrust
of too-much government, a desire to protect
the integrity of the dollar by reducing inflation - and it was on this platform that the
president took his cause to the people. The
State of the Union Address therefore not
only sounded bicentennial echoes but also
established his platform priorities for the
upcoming campaign.

Source: New York Times,
January 20, 1976

As we begin our Bicentennial, America is still one of the youngest nations in recorded history. Long before our forefathers came to these
shores, men and women had been struggling on this planet to forge a better life for themselves and their families.

In man's long upward march from savagery and slavery -- throughout
the nearly 2,000 years of the Christian calendar, the nearly 6,000 years
of Jewish reckoning -- there have been many deep, terrifying valleys, but
also many bright and towering peaks.

One peak stands highest in the ranges of human history. One example
shines forth of a people uniting to produce abundance and to share the good
life fairly and with freedom. One union holds out the promise of justice
and opportunity for every citizen.

That Union is the United States of America.

We have not remade paradise on earth. We know perfection will not
be found here. But think for a minute how far we have come in 200 years.

We came from many roots and we have many branches. Yet all
Americans across the eight generations that separate us from the stirring
deeds of 1776, those who know no other homeland and those who just found
refuge among our shores, say in unison:

I am proud of America and I'm proud to be an American. Life will
be better here for my children than for me.

I believe this not because I am told to believe it, but because life has
been better for me than it was for my father and my mother.

I know it will be better for my children because my hands, my brains,
my voice and my vote, can help make it happen.

It can happen here in America.

It has happened to you and to me.

Government exists to create and preserve conditions in which people 'can translate their ideals into practical reality. In the best of times, much is lost in translation. But we try.

Sometimes we have tried and failed.

Always we've had the best of intentions. But in the recent past we sometimes forgot the sound principles that guided us through most of our history. We wanted to accomplish great things and solve age-old problems. And we became overconfident of our abilities. We tried to be a policeman abroad and the indulgent parent here at home. We thought we could transform the country through massive national programs.

-- But often the programs did not work; too often, they only made things worse.

-- In our rush to accomplish great deeds quickly, we trampled on sound principles of restraint, and endangered the rights of individuals.

-- We unbalanced our economic system by the huge and unprecedented growth of Federal expenditures and borrowing. And we were not totally honest with ourselves about how much these programs would cost and how we would pay for them.

-- Finally, we shifted our emphasis from defense to domestic problems while our adversaries continued a massive buildup of arms.

The time has now come for a fundamentally different approach for a new realism that is true to the great principles upon which this nation was founded.

We must introduce a new balance to our economy -- a balance that favors not only sound, active government but also a much more vigorous, healthier economy that can create new jobs and hold down prices.

We must introduce a new balance in the relationship between the individual and the Government -- a balance that favors greater individual freedom and self-reliance.

We must strike a new balance in our system of federalism -- a balance that favors greater responsibility and freedom for the leaders of our states and local governments.

We must introduce a new balance between the spending on domestic programs and spending on defense -- a balance that insures we will fully meet our obligations to the needy while also protecting our security in a world that is still hostile to freedom.

And in all that we do, we must be more honest with the American people; promising them no more than we can deliver, and delivering all that we promise.

The genius of America has been its incredible ability to improve the lives of its citizens through a unique combination of governmental and free citizen activity.

History and experience tell us that moral progress cannot come in comfortable and in complacent times, but out of trial and out of confusion.

Tom Paine aroused the troubled Americans of 1776 to stand up to the times that try men's souls, because the harder the conflict the more glorious the triumph.

Just a year ago I reported that the state of the Union was not good.

Tonight I report that the state of our Union is better -- in many ways a lot better -- but still not good enough.

To paraphrase Tom Paine, 1975 was not a year for summer soldiers and sunshine patriots. It was a year of fears and alarms and of dire forecasts -- most of which never happened and won't happen.

As you recall, the year 1975 opened with rancor and with bitterness. Political misdeeds of the past had neither been forgotten nor forgiven.

The longest, most divisive war in our history was winding toward an unhappy conclusion. Many feared that the end of that foreign war of men and machines meant the beginning of a domestic war of recrimination and reprisal.

Friends and adversaries abroad were asking whether America had lost its nerve.

Finally, our economy was ravaged by inflation -- inflation that was plunging us into the worst recession in four decades.

At the same time, Americans became increasingly alienated from big institutions. They were steadily losing confidence not just in big government, but in big business, big labor and big education, among others.

Ours was a troubled land.

And so, 1975 was a year of hard decisions, difficult compromises, and a new realism that taught us something important about America.

It brought back a needed measure of common sense, steadfastness and self-discipline. Americans did not panic or demand instant but useless cures. In all sectors people met their difficult problems with restraint and responsibility worthy of their great heritage.

Add up the separate pieces of progress in 1975, subtract the setbacks, and the sum total shows that we are not only headed in a new direction, a direction which I proposed 12 months ago, but it turned out to be the right direction.

It is the right direction because it follows the truly revolutionary American concept of 1776 which holds that in a free society, the making of public policy and successful problem-solving involves much more than government. It involves a full partnership among all branches and all levels of government, private institutions and individual citizens.

Common sense tells me to stick to that steady course.

Take the state of our economy.

Last January most things were rapidly getting worse.

This January most things are slowly but surely getting better.

The worst recession since World War II turned around in April. The best cost of living news of the past year is that double-digit inflation of 12 percent or higher was cut almost in half. The worst -- unemployment remains far too high. . . .

My first objective is to have sound economic growth without inflation.

We all know from recent experience what runaway inflation does to ruin every other worthy purpose. We are slowing it; we must stop it cold.

For many Americans the way to a healthy noninflationary economy has become increasingly apparent; the Government must stop spending so much and stop borrowing so much of our money; more money must remain in private hands where it will do the most good. To hold down the cost of living, we must hold down the cost of government.

In the past decade, the Federal budget has been growing at an average rate of over 10 percent a year. The budget I am submitting Wednesday cuts this rate of growth in half. I have kept my promise to submit a budget for the next fiscal year of $395 billion. In fact, it is $394.2 billion.

By holding down the growth of Federal spending, we can afford additional tax cuts and return to the people who pay taxes more decision-making power over their own lives. . . .

Five out of six jobs in this country are in private business and industry. Common sense tells us this is the place to look for more jobs and to find them faster.

I mean real, rewarding, permanent jobs.

To achieve this we must offer the American people greater incentives to invest in the future. My tax proposals are a major step in that direction.

To supplement these proposals, I ask that Congress enact changes in Federal tax laws that will speed up plant expansion and the purchase of new equipment. My recommendations will concentrate this job-creation tax incentive in areas where the unemployment rate now runs over 7 percent. Legislation to get this started must be approved at the earliest possible date.

Within the strict budget total that I will recommend for the coming year, I will ask for additional housing assistance for 500,000 families. These programs will expand housing opportunities, spur construction and help to house moderate and low income families. . . .

A necessary condition of a healthy economy is freedom from the petty tyranny of massive government regulation . We are wasting literally millions of working hours costing billions of taxpayers' and consumers' dollars because of bureaucratic red tape. The American farmer, who now feeds 215 million American and also millions worldwide, has shown how much more he can produce without the shackles of government controls.

Now, we badly need reforms in other key areas in our economy -- the airlines, trucking, railroads and financial institutions. I have submitted concrete plans in each of these areas, not to help this or that industry, but to foster competition and to bring prices down for the consumer.

This Administration will strictly enforce the Federal antitrust laws for the very same purposes.

Taking a longer look at America's future, there can be neither sustaining growth nor more jobs unless we continue to have an assured supply of energy to run our economy. Domestic production of oil and gas is still declining. Our dependence on foreign oil at high prices is still too great, draining jobs and dollars away from our own economy at the rate of $125 per year for every American.

Last month I signed a compromise national energy bill which enacts a part of my comprehensive energy independence program. This legislation was later, not the complete answer to energy independence, but still a start in the right direction.

I again urge the Congress to move ahead immediately on the remainder of my energy proposals to make America invulnerable to the foreign oil cartel. . . .

Hospital and medical services in America are among the best in the world, but the cost of a serious and extended illness can quickly wipe out a family's lifetime savings. Increasing health costs are of deep concern to all and a powerful force pushing up the cost of living.

The burden of catastrophic illness can be borne by very few in our society. We must eliminate this fear from every family.

I propose catastrophic health insurance for everybody covered by Medicare. To finance this added protection, fees for short-term care will go up somewhat, but nobody after reaching age 65 will have to pay more than $500 a year for covered hospital or nursing home care nor more than $250 for one year's doctor's bills.

We cannot realistically afford federally dictated national health insurance providing full coverage for all 215 million Americans. The experience of other countries raises questions about the quality as well as the cost of such plans. But I do envision the day when we may use the private health insurance system to offer more middle income families high quality health services at prices they can afford and shield them also from their catastrophic illnesses.

Using resources now available, I propose improving the Medicare and other Federal health programs to help those who really need protection; older people and the poor. . . .

I am concerned about the integrity of our Social Security trust fund that enables people -- those retired and those still working who will retire -- to count on this source of retirement income. Younger workers watch their deductions rise and wonder if they will be adequately protected in the future.

We must meet this challenge head-on.

Simple arithmetic warns all of us that the Social Security trust fund is headed for trouble. Unless we act soon to make sure the fund takes in as much as it pays out, there will be no security for old or for young.

I must therefore recommend a three-tenths of 1 percent increase in both employer and employee Social Security taxes effective Jan. 1, 1977. This will cost each covered employee less than one extra dollar a week and will insure the integrity of the trust fund.

As we rebuild our economy, we have a continuing responsibility to provide a temporary cushion to the unemployed. At my request the Congress enacted two extensions and two expansions in unemployment insurance, which helped those who were jobless during 1975. These programs will continue in 1976.

In my fiscal year 1977 budget, I am also requesting funds to continue proven job training and employment opportunity programs for millions of other Americans.

Compassion and a sense of community -- two of America's greatest strengths through our history -- tell us we must take care of our neighbors who cannot take care of themselves. The host of Federal programs in this field reflect our generosity as a people.

But everyone realizes that when it comes to welfare, government at all levels is not doing the job well. Too many of our welfare programs are inequitable and invite abuse. Too many of our welfare programs have problems from beginning to end. Worse, we are wasting badly needed resources without reaching many of the truly needy.

Complex welfare programs cannot be reformed overnight. Surely we cannot simply dump welfare into the laps of the 50 states, their local taxpayers or private charities, and just walk away from it. Not is it the right time for massive and sweeping changes while we are still recovering from the recession.

Nevertheless, there are still plenty of improvements that we can make. I will ask Congress for Presidential authority to tighten up the rules for eligibility and benefits. . . .

Protecting the life and property of the citizen at home is the responsibility of all public officials but is primarily the job of local and state law enforcement authority.

Americans have always found the very thought of a Federal police force repugnant, and so do I. But there are proper ways in which we can help to insure domestic tranquillity as the Constituion charges us.

My recommendations on how to control violent crime were submitted to the Congress last June with strong emphasis on protecting the innocent victims of crime.

To keep a convicted criminal from committing more crimes we must put him in prison so he cannot harm more law-abiding citizens. To be effective, this punishment must be swift and it must be certain.

Too often criminals are not sent to prison after conviction but are allowed to return to the streets.

Some judges are reluctant to send convicted criminals to prison because of inadequate facilities. To alleviate this problem at the Federal level, my new budget proposes the construction of four new Federal facilities.

To speed Federal justice, I propose an increase this year in United States attorneys prosecuting Federal crimes and reinforcement of the number of United States marshals.

Additional Federal judges are needed, as recommended by me and the Judicial Conference.

Another major threat to every American's person and property is the criminal carrying a handgun. The way to cut down on the criminal use of guns is not to take guns away from the law-abiding citizen but to impose mandatory sentences for crimes in which a gun is used, make it harder to obtain cheap guns for criminal purposes, and concentrate gun control enforcement in high crime areas.

My budget recommends 500 additional Federal agents in the 11 largest metropolitan high crime areas to help local authorities stop criminals from selling and using handguns.

The sale of hard drugs is tragically on the increase again. I have rirected (sic) all agencies of the Federal Government to step up law enforcement efforts against those who deal in drugs. In 1975, I'm glad to report, Federal agents seized substantially more heroin coming into our country than in 1974.

I recommended months ago that the Congress enact mandatory fixed sentences for persons convicted of Federal crimes involving the sale of hard drugs. Hard drugs, we all know, degrade the spirit as they destroy the body of their users. . . .

The protection of the lives and property of Americans from foreign enemies is one of my primary responsibilities as President.

In a world of instant communications and intercontinental ballistic missiles, in a world economy that is global and interdependent, our relations with other nations become more, not less, important to the lives of Americans.

America has had a unique role in the world since the day of our independence 200 years ago. And ever since the end of World War II, we have borne -- successfully -- a heavy responsibility for insuring a stable world order and hope for human progress.

Today, the state of our foreign policy is sound and strong.

-- We are at peace -- and I will do all in my power to keep it that way.

-- Our military forces are capable and ready; our military power is without equal. And I intend to keep it that way.

Our principal alliances, with the industrial democracies of the Atlantic Community and Japan, have never been more solid.

-- A further agreement to limit the strategic arms race may be achieved.

-- We have an improving relationship with China, the world's most populous nation.

-- The key elements for peace among the nations of the Middle East now exist.

-- Our traditional friendships in Latin America, Africa, and Asia continue.

-- We have taken the role of leadership in launching a serious and hopeful dialogue between the industrial world and the developing world.

-- We have helped to achieve significant reform of the international monetary system.

We should be proud of what America, what our country has accomplished in these areas, and I believe the American people are.

The American people have heard too much about how terrible our mistakes, how evil our deeds, and how misguided our purposes. The American people know better.

The truth is we are the world's greatest democracy. We remain the symbol of man's aspirations for liberty and well-being. We are the embodiment of hope for progress.

I say it's time we quit downgrading ourselves as a nation. Of course, it's our responsibility to learn the right lessons from past mistakes. It is our duty to see that they never happen again. But our greater duty is to look to the future. The world's troubles will not go away. . . .

The defense budget I will submit to the Congress for fiscal year 1977 will show an essential increase over the current year. It provides for a real growth in purchasing power over this year's defense budget, which includes the cost of the all-volunteer force.

We are continuing to make economies to enhance the efficiency of our military forces. But the budget I will submit represents the necessity of American strength for the real world in which we live.

As conflict and rivalry persist in the world, our United States intelligence capabilities must be the best in the world.

The crippling of our foreign intelligence services increases the danger of American involvement in direct armed conflict. Our adversaries are encouraged to adopt or attempt new adventures, while our own abilty to monitor them, and to influence events short of military action, is undermined.

Without effective intelligence capability, the United States stands blindfolded and hobbled.

In the near future, I will take actions to reform and strengthen our intelligence community. I ask for your positive cooperation. It is time to go beyond sensationalism and insure an effective, responsible and responsive intelligence capability.

Tonight I have spoken of our problems at home and abroad. I have recommended policies that will meet the challenge of our third century.

I have no doubt that our Union will endure -- better, stronger and with more individual freedom.

We can see forward only dimly -- one year, five years, a generation perhaps.

Like our forefathers, we know that if we meet the challenges of our own time with a common sense of purpose and conviction -- if we remain true to our Constitution and to our ideals -- then we can know that the future will be better than the past.

I see America today crossing a threshold, not just because it is our Bicentennial, but because we have been tested in adversity. We have taken a new look at what we want to be and what we want our nation to become.

I see America resurgent, certain once again that life will be better for our children than it is for us, seeking strength that cannot be counted in megatons and riches that cannot be eroded by inflation.

I see these United States of America moving forward as before toward a more perfect Union where the Government serves and the people rule.

We will not make this happen simply by making speeches, good or bad, yours or mine, but by hard work and hard decisions made with courage and common sense.

I have heard many inspiring Presidential speeches, but the words I remember best were spoken by Dwight D. Eisenhower.

"America is not good because it is great," the President said. "America is great because it is good."

President Eisenhower was raised in a poor but religious home in the heart of America. His simple words echoed President Lincoln's eloquent testament that "right makes might." And Lincoln in turn evoked the silent image of George Washington kneeling in prayer at Valley Forge.

So all these magic memories, which link eight generations of Americans, are summed up in the inscription just above me.

How many times have we seen it? -- "In God We Trust."

Let us engrave it now in each of our hearts as we begin our Bicentennial.

FORD ACCEPTS THE REPUBLICAN NOMINATION
AUGUST 19, 1976

Shortly after America's Bicentennial bash of
July 4, 1976, the Democratic party nominated
Jimmy Carter, the former governor of Georgia,
as their presidential condidate. Some polls
showed Ford to be thirty points behind Carter
and the president was not even certain of winning his own party's nomination. Nevertheless,
by the time the Republicans met in Kansas City,
Ford had secured the necessary number of delegates and was assured of nomination. Already
he had cut into Carter's seemingly insurmount-
able lead. Ford's acceptance speech was perhaps
his finest political moment. Not only did the
address invigorate the G.O.P., but also it specif-
ically challenged Carter to a series of presidential
debates that may have long-lasting effects on our
politics.

Source: Weekly Compilation of Presidential Documents:
Gerald R. Ford, 1976, V 12, #34, 1267-1272.

I am honored by your nomination, and I accept it with pride, with gratitude, and with a total will to win a great victory for the American people.
We will wage a winning campaign in every region of this country, from
the snowy banks of Minnesota to the sandy plains of Georgia. We concede
not a single State. We concede not a single vote.

This evening I am proud to stand before this great convention as the
first incumbent President since Dwight D. Eisenhower who can tell the
American people: America is at peace.

Tonight, I can tell you straightaway this Nation is sound, this Nation
is secure, this Nation is on the march to full economic recovery and a
better quality of life for all Americans.

And I will tell you one more thing. This year the issues are on our
side. I am ready, I am eager to go before the American people and debate the real issues face to face with Jimmy Carter. The American people have a right to know firsthand exactly where both of us stand.

I am deeply grateful to those who stood with me in winning the nomination of the party whose cause I have served all of my adult life. I respect the convictions of those who want a change in Washington. I want a
change, too. After 22 long years of majority misrule, let's change the
United States Congress.

My gratitude tonight reaches far beyond this arena to countless friends
whose confidence, hard work, and unselfish support have brought me to

this moment. It would be unfair to single out anyone, but may I make an exception for my wonderful family --Mike, Jack, Steve and Susan, and especially my dear wife Betty.

We Republicans have had some tough competition. We not only preach the virtues of competition, we practice them. But tonight we come together not on a battlefield to conclude a cease-fire, but to join forces on a training field that has conditioned us all for the rugged contest ahead.

Let me say this from the bottom of my heart. After the scrimmages of the past few months, it really feels good to have Ron Reagan on the same side of the line.

To strengthen our championship lineup, the convention has wisely chosen one of the ablest Americans as our next Vice President, Senator Bob Dole of Kansas. With his help, with your help, with the help of millions of Americans who cherish peace, who want freedom preserved, prosperity shared, and pride in America, we will win this election.

I speak not of a Republican victory, but a victory for the American people. You at home listening tonight, you are the people who pay the taxes and obey the laws. You are the people who make our system work. You are the people who make America what it is. It is from your ranks that I come and on your side that I stand.

Something wonderful happened to this country of ours the past 2 years. We all came to realize it on the Fourth of July. Together, out of years of turmoil and tragedy, wars and riots, assassinations and wrong-doing in high places, Americans recaptured the Spirit of 1776. We saw again the pioneer vision of our revolutionary founders and our immigrant ancestors. Their vision was of free men and free women enjoying limited government and unlimited opportunity.

The mandate I want in 1976 is to make this vision a reality, but it will take the voices and the votes of many more Americans who are not Republicans to make that mandate binding and my mission possible.

I have been called an unelected President, an accidental President. We may even hear that again from the other party, despite the fact that I was welcomed and endorsed by an overwhelming majority of their elected representatives in the Congress who certified my fitness to our highest office.

Having become Vice President and President without expecting or seeking either, I have a special feeling toward these high offices. To me, the Presidency and the Vice Presidency were not prizes to be won, but a duty to be done.

So, tonight, it is not the power and the glamor of the Presidency that leads me to ask for another 4 years. It is something every hard-working American will understand --the challenge of a job well begun, but far from finished.

Two years ago, on August 9, 1974, I placed my hand on the Bible, which Betty held, and took the same constitutional oath that was administered to George Washington. I had faith in our people, in our institutions, and in myself.

"My fellow Americans, " I said, "our long national nightmare is over. "
It was an hour in our history that troubled our minds and tore at our hearts.
Anger and hatred had risen to dangerous levels, dividing friends and
families. The polarization of our political order had aroused unworthy
passions of reprisal and revenge. Our governmental system was closer
to stalemate than at any time since Abraham Lincoln took that same oath
of office.

Our economy was in the throes of runaway inflation, taking us head-
long into the worst recession since Franklin D. Roosevelt took the same
oath. On that dark day I told my fellow countrymen, "I am acutely aware
that you have not elected me as your President by your ballots, so I ask
you to confirm me as your President with your prayers. "

On a marble fireplace in the White House is carved a prayer which
John Adams wrote. It concludes, "May none but honest and wise men ever
rule under this roof. " Since I have resided in that historic house, I have
tried to live by that prayer. I faced many tough problems. I probably
made some mistakes, but on balance. America and Americans have made
an incredible comeback since August 1974. Nobody can honestly say other-
wise. And the plain truth is that the great progress we have made at home
and abroad was in spite of the majority who run the Congress of the United
States.

For 2 years I have stood for all the people against a vote-hungry,
free-spending congressional majority on Capitol Hill. Fifty-five times
I vetoed extravagant and unwise legislation; 45 times I made those vetoes
stick. Those vetoes have saved American taxpayers billions and billions
of dollars. I am against the big tax spender and for the little taxpayer.

I called for a permanent tax cut, coupled with spending reductions,
to stimulate the economy and relieve hard-pressed middle-income taxpayers. Your personal exemption must be raised from $750 to $1,000. The
other party's platform talks about tax reform, but there is one big problem -- their own Congress won't act.

I called for reasonable constitutional restrictions on court-ordered
busing of schoolchildren, but the other party's platform concedes that
busing should be a last resort. But there is the same problem --their
own Congress won't act.

I called for a major overhaul of criminal laws to crack down on crime
and illegal drugs The other party's platform deplores America's $90
billion cost of crime. There is the problem again -- their own Congress
won't act.

The other party's platform talks about a strong defense. Now, here
is the other side of the problem -- their own Congress did act. They
slashed $50 billion from our national defense needs in the last 10 years.

My friends, Washington is not the problem their Congress is the
problem.

You know, the President of the United States is not a magician who can wave a wand or sign a paper that will instantly end a war, cure a recession, or make bureaucracy disappear. A President has immense powers under the Constitution, but all of them ultimately come from the American people and their mandate to him.

That is why, tonight, I turn to the American people and ask not only for your prayers, but also for your strength and your support, for your voice and for your vote. I come before you with a 2-year record of performance, without your mandate. I offer you a 4-year pledge of greater performance with your mandate.

As Governor Al Smith used to say, "Let's look at the record." Two years ago, inflation was 12 percent. Sales were off. Plants were shut down. Thousands were being laid off every week. Fear of the future was throttling down our economy and threatening millions of families.

Let's look at the record since August 1974. Inflation has been cut in half. Payrolls are up. Profits are up. Production is up. Purchases are up. Since the recession was turned around almost 4 million of our fellow Americans have found new jobs or got their old jobs back. This year, more men and women have jobs than ever before in the history of the United States. Confidence has returned and we are in the full surge of sound recovery to steady prosperity.

Two years ago America was mired in withdrawal from Southeast Asia. A decade of Congresses had shortchanged our global defenses and threatened our strategic posture. Mounting tension between Israel and the Arab nations made another war seem inevitable. The whole world watched and wondered where America was going. Did we in our domestic turmoil have the will, the stamina, and the unity to stand up for freedom?

Look at the record since August, 2 years ago. Today, America is at peace and seeks peace for all nations. Not a single American is at war anywhere on the face of this Earth tonight.

Our ties with Western Europe and Japan, economic as well as military, were never stronger. Our relations with Eastern Europe, the Soviet Union, and mainland China are firm, vigilant, and forward-looking. Policies I have initiated offer sound progress for the peoples of the Pacific, Africa, and Latin America. Israel and Egypt, both trusting the United States, have taken an historic step that promises an eventual just settlement for the whole Middle East.

The world now respects America's policy of peace through strength. The United States is again the confident leader of the free world. Nobody questions our dedication to peace, but nobody doubts our willingness to use strength when our vital interests are at stake, and we will.

I called for an up-to-date, powerful Army, Navy, Air Force, and Marines that will keep America secure for decades. A strong military posture is always the best insurance for peace. But America's strength has never rested on arms alone. It is rooted in our mutual commitment of our citizens and leaders in the highest standards of ethics and morality and in the spiritual renewal which our Nation is undergoing right now.

Two years ago, people's confidence in their highest officials, to whom they had overwhelmingly entrusted power, had twice been shattered. Losing faith in the word of their elected leaders, Americans lost some of their own faith in themselves.

Again, let's look at the record since August 1974. From the start, my administration has been open, candid, forthright. While my entire public and private life was under searching examination for theVice Presidency, I reaffirmed my life-long conviction that truth is the glue that holds government together -- not only government but civilization, itself. I have demanded honesty, decency, and personal integrity from everybody in the executive branch of the Government. The House and Senate have the same duty.

The American people will not accept a double standard in the United States Congress. Those who make our laws today must not debase the reputation of our great legislative bodies that have given us such giants as Daniel Webster, Henry Clay, Sam Rayburn, and Robert A. Taft. Whether in the Nation's Capital, the State capital, or city hall, private morality and public trust must go together.

From August of 1974 to August of 1976, the record shows steady progress upward toward prosperity, peace, and public trust. My record is one of progress, not platitudes. My record is one of specifics, not smiles. My record is one of performance, not promises. It is a record I am proud to run on. It is a record the American people -- Democrats, Independents, and Republicans alike -- will support on November 2.

For the next 4 years I pledge to you that I will hold to the steady course we have begun. But I have no intention of standing on the record alone. We will continue winning the fight against inflation. We will go on reducing the dead weight and impudence of bureaucracy.

We will submit a balanced budget by 1978. We will improve the quality of life at work, at play, and in our homes and in our neighborhoods. We will not abandon our cities. We will encourage urban programs which assure safety in the streets, create healthy environments, and restore neighborhood pride.

We will return control of our children's education to parents and local school authorities. We will make sure that the party of Lincoln remains the party of equal rights. We will create a tax structure that is fair for all our citizens, one that preserves the continuity of the family home, the family farm, and the family business.

We will ensure the integrity of the social security system and improve Medicare so that our older citizens can enjoy the health and the happiness that they have earned. There is no reason they should have to go broke just to get well.

We will make sure that this rich Nation does not neglect citizens who are less fortunate, but provides for their needs with compassion and with dignity. We will reduce the growth and the cost of government and allow

individual breadwinners and businesses to keep more of the money that
they earn.

We will create a climate in which our economy will provide a meaningful job for everyone who wants to work and a decent standard of life
for all Americans. We will ensure that all of our young people have a
better chance in life than we had, an education they can use, and a career
they can be proud of.

We will carry out a farm policy that assures a fair market price for
the farmer, encourages full production, leads to record exports, and eases
the hunger within the human family. We will never use the bounty of
America's farmers as a pawn in international diplomacy. There will be
no embargoes.

We will continue our strong leadership to bring peace, justice, and
economic progress where there is turmoil, especially in the Middle East.
We will build a safer and saner world through patient negotiations and
dependable arms agreements which reduce the danger of conflict and hor-
ror of thermonuclear war. While I am President, we will not return to a
collision course that could reduce civilization to ashes.

We will build an America where people feel rich in spirit as well as in
worldly goods. We will build an America where people feel rich in spirit
as well as in worldly goods. We will build an America where people feel
proud about themselves and about their country.

We will build on performance, not promises; experience, not expedi-
ency; real progress instead of mysterious plans to be revealed in some
dim and distant future.

The American people are wise, wiser than our opponents think. They
know who pays for every campaign promise. They are not afraid of the
truth. We will tell them the truth.

From start to finish, our campaign will be credible; it will be responsible. We will come out fighting, and we will win. Yes, we have all seen
the polls and the pundits who say our party is dead. I have heard that before. So did Harry Truman. I will tell you what I think. The only polls
that count are the polls the American people go to on November 2.

And right now, I predict that the American people are going to say
that night, "Jerry, you have done a good job, keep right on doing it."

As I try in my imagination to look into the homes where families are
watching the end of this great convention, I can't tell which faces are Republicans, which are Democrats, and which are Independents. I cannot see
their color or their creed. I see only Americans.

I see Americans who love their husbands, their wives, and their children. I see Americans who love their country for what it has been and what
it must become. I see Americans who work hard, but who are willing to
sacrifice all they have worked for to keep their children and their country
free.

I see Americans who in their own quiet way pray for peace among nations
and peace among themselves. We do love our neighbors, and we do forgive

those who have trepassed against us.

I see a new generation that knows what is right and knows itself, a generation determined to preserve its ideals, its environment, our Nation, and the world.

My fellow Americans, I like what I see. I have no fear for the future of this great country. And as we go forward together, I promise you once more what I promised before: to uphold the Constitution, to do what is right as God gives me to see the right, and to do the very best that I can for America.

God helping me, I won't let you down.

FORD vs. CARTER - THE SECOND DEBATE
OCTOBER 6, 1976

Carter readily accepted the president's debate challenge. In their first encounter, on
September 23, most observers believed Ford
had a slight edge and expected him to expand
on that margin in the October 6 discussion of
foreign affairs. However, during the course
of that debate, the president seriously erred
while speaking of Eastern Europe and Carter
quickly took advantage of the gaffe. Perhaps
more damaging than the error itself was Ford's
refusal to acknowledge it as such; for several
crucial days his campaign completely bogged
down.

Source: New York Times,
October 7, 1976.

Q. Mr. President, I'd like to explore a little more deeply our relationship with the Russians. They used to brag back in Krushchiev's day
that because of their greater patience and because of our greed for business deals that they would sooner or later get the better of us. Is it possible that despite some setbacks in the Middle East, they've proved their
point? Our allies in France and Italy are now flirting with communism.
We've recognized the permanent Communist regime in East Germany.
We've virtually signed in Helsinki an agreement that the Russians have
dominance in Eastern Europe. We've bailed out Soviet agriculture with
our huge grain sales. We've given them large loans, access to our best
technology and if the Senate hadn't interfered with the Jackson Amendment,
maybe you would have given them even larger loans. Is that what you call
a two-way street of traffic in Europe?

FORD: I believe that we have negotiated with the Soviet Union since
I've been President from a position of strength. And let me cite several
examples.

Shortly after I became President in December of 1974, I met with General Secretary Brezhnev in Vlodivostok and we agreed to a mutual cap on
the ballistic missile launcher at a ceiling of 2,400 which means that the
Soviet Union, if that becomes a permanent agreement, will have to make
a reduction in their launchers that they now have or plan to have.

I negotiated at Vladivostok with Mr. Brezhnev a limitation on the
MIRVing of their ballistic missiles at a figure of 1,320 which is the first
time that any President has achieved a cap either on launchers or on MIRV's.

It seems to me that we can go from there to grain sales. The grain sales have been a benefit to American agriculture. We have achieved a five and three-quarter-year sale of a minimum six million metric tons, which means that they have already bought about four million metric tons this year and are bound to buy another two million metric tons to take the grain and corn and wheat that the American farmers have produced in order to have full production and these grain sales to the Soviet Union have helped us tremendously in meeting the costs of the additional oil -- the oil that we have bought from overseas.

If we turn to Helsinki -- I'm glad you raised it Mr. Frankel. In the case of Helsinki, 35 nations signed an agreement, including the Secretary of State for the Vatican. I can't under any circumstances believe that the -- His Holiness, the Pope -- would agree by signing that agreement that the 35 nations have turned over to the Warsaw Pact nations the domination of Eastern Europe. It just isn't true. And if Mr. Carter alleges that His Holiness by signing that has done, he is totally inaccurate.

And what has been accomplished by the Helsinki agreement? No. 1, we have an agreement where they notify us and we notify them of any military maneuvers that are to be undertaken. They have done it. In both cases where they've done so, there is no Soviet domination of Eastern Europe and there never will be under a Ford Administration.

MODERATOR: Governor Carter?

Q: I'm sorry, could I just follow -- did I understand you to say, sir, that the Russians are not using Eastern Europe as their own sphere of influence in occupying most of the countries there and making sure with their troops that it's a Communist zone, whereas on our side of line the Italians and the French are still flirting with. . .

FORD: I don't believe, Mr. Frankel, that the Yugoslavians consider themselves dominated by the Soviet Union. I don't believe that the Rumanians consider themselves dominated by the Soviet Union. I don't believe that the Poles consider themselves dominated by the Soviet Union.

Each of those countries is independent, autonomous, it has its own territorial integrity and the United States does not concede that those countries are under the domination of the Soviet Union. As a matter of fact, I visited Poland, Yugoslavia and Rumania to make certain that the people of those countries understood that the President of the United States and the people of the United States are dedicated to their independence, their autonomy and their freedom....

THE STATE OF THE UNION
JANUARY 12, 1977

> After one of the closest races in American
> history, Gerald Ford yielded the presidency
> to James Earl Carter. Despite his valiant
> comeback, the president had lost an election
> for the first time. In January, 1977, Ford
> delivered his third and last State of the Union
> message; he used the opportunity to make a
> valedictory statement. Few Americans who
> lived through his troubled presidency can
> doubt that he did achieve for us a "more per-
> fect Union."

> Source: New York Times,
> January 13, 1977.

In accordance with the Constitution, I come before you once again
to report on the State of the Union.

This report will be my last, maybe.

But for the Union, it is only the first of such reports in our third
century of independence, the close of which none of us will ever see. We
can be confident, however, that 100 years from now a freely elected President will come before a freely elected Congress, chosen to renew our
great republic's pledge to government of the people, by the people and for
the people.

For my part, I pray the third century we are beginning will bring to
all Americans, our children and their children's children, a greater measure of individual equality, opportunity and justice, a greater abundance
of spiritual and material blessings, and a higher quality of life, liberty
and the pursuit of happiness.

The State of the Union is a measurement of the many elements of
which it is composed -- a political union of diverse states, an economic
union of varying interests, an intellectual union of common convictions
and a moral union of immutable ideals.

Taken in sum, I can report that the State of the Union is good. There
is room for improvement as always, but today we have a more perfect
union than when my stewardship began.

As a people, we discovered that our Bicentennial was much more
than a celebration of the past; it became a joyous reaffirmation of all
that it means to be Americans, a confirmation before all the world of the
bitality and durability of our free institutions.

I am proud to have been privileged to preside over the affairs of our
Federal Government during these eventful years when we proved, as I

said in my first words upon assuming office, that "our Constitution works; our great republic is a Government of laws and not of men; here, the people rule."

The people have spoken; they have chosen a new President and a new Congress to work their will; I congratulate you -- particularly the new members --as sincerely as I did President-elect Carter. In a few days, it will be his duty to outline for you his priorities and legislative recommendations. Tonight, I will not infringe on that responsibility, but rather wish him the very best in all that is good for our country. . . .

Because the transfer of authority in our form of government affects the state of the union, and of the world, I am happy to report to you that the current transition is proceeding very well. I was determined that it should; I wanted the new President to get off on an easier start than I had.

When I became President on August 9, 1974, our nation was deeply divided and tormented. In rapid succession, the Vice President and the President had resigned in disgrace. We were still struggling with the after-effects of a long, unpopular and bloody war in Southeast Asia.

The economy was unstable and racing toward the worst recession in 40 years. People were losing jobs. The cost of living was soaring. The Congress and the chief executive were at loggerheads. The integrity of our constitutional process and of other institutions was being questioned.

For more than 15 years, domestic spending had soared as Federal programs multiplied and the expense escalated annually. During the same period, our national security needs were steadily shortchanged.

In the grave situation which prevailed in August 1974, our will to maintain our international leadership was in doubt.

I asked for your prayers, and went to work.

In January 1975, I reported to the Congress that the state of the union was not good. I proposed urgent action to improve the economy and to achieve energy independence in ten years I reassured America's allies and sought to reduce the danger of confrontation with potential adversaries. I pledged a new direction for America.

Nineteen seventy-five was a year of difficult decisions, but Americans responded with realism, common sense and self-discipline.

By January 1976, we were headed in a new direction, which I hold to be the right direction for a free society. It was guided by the belief that successful problem-solving requires more than Federal action alone; that it involves a full partnership among all branches and all levels of government, and public policies which nurture and promote the creative energies of private enterprises, institutions and individual citizens.

A year ago, I reported that the state of the union was better -- in many ways a lot better -- but still not good enough.

Common sense told me to stick to the steady course we were on, to continue to restrain the inflationary growth of government, to reduce taxes as well as spending, to return local decisions to local officials to provide for long-range sufficiency in energy and national security needs.

I resisted the immense pressures of an election year to open the floodgates of Federal money and the temptation to promise more than I could deliver. I told it as it was to the American people and demonstrated to the world that, in our spirited political competition, as in this chamber, Americans can disagree without being disagreeable.

Now, after 30 months as your President, I can say that while we still have a way to go, I am proud of the long way we have come together.

I am proud of the part I have had in rebuilding confidence in the Presidency, confidence in our free system and confidence in our future. Once again, Americans believe in themselves, in their leaders, and in the promise that tomorrow holds for their children.

I am proud that today America is at peace. None of our sons are fighting and dying in battle anywhere in the world. And the chance for peace among all nations is improved by our determination to honor our vital commitments in defense of peace and freedom.

I am proud that the United States has strong defenses, strong alliances and a sound courageous foreign policy.

Our alliances with major partners, the great industrial democracies of Western Europe, Japan, and Canada have never been more solid. Consultations on mutual security, defense and East-West relations have grown closer. Collaboration has branched out into new fields, such as energy, economic policy and relations with the Third World.

We have used many avenues for cooperation, including summit meetings held among major allied countries. The friendship of the democracies is deeper, warmer and more effective than at any time in 30 years.

We are maintaining stability in the strategic nuclear balance, and pushing back the spectre of nuclear war. A decisive step forward was taken in the Vladivostok accord which I negotiated with General Secretary Brezhnev -- joint recognition that an equal ceiling should be placed on the number of strategic weapons on each side.

With resolve and wisdom on the part of both nations, a good agreement is well within reach this year.

The framework for peace in the Middle East has been built. Hopes for future progress in the Middle East were stirred by the historic agreements we reached and the trust and confidence that we formed. . .

American leadership has helped to stimulate new international efforts to stem the proliferation of nuclear weapons and to shape a comprehensive treaty governing the use of the oceans.

I am gratified by these accomplishments. They constitute a record of broad success for America, and for the peace and prosperity of all mankind. This Administration leaves to its successor a world in better condition that we found. We leave, as well, a solid foundation for progress on a range of issues that are vital to the well being of America.

What has been achieved in the field of foreign affairs, and what can be accomplished by the new administration, demonstrate the genius of

Americans working together for the common good. It is this, our remark-
able ability to work together, that has made us a unique nation. It is Congress, the President, and the people striving for a better world.

I know all patriotic Americans want this nation's foreign policy to
succeed.

I urge members of my party in the Congress to give the new President
loyal support in this area. . . .

At home, I am encouraged by the nation's recovery from the recession and our steady return to sound economic growth. It is now continuing after the recent period of uncertainty, which is part of the price we
pay for free elections.

Our most pressing need today and in the future is more jobs -- productive and permanent jobs created by a thriving economy.

We must revise our tax system both to ease the burden of heavy tax-
ation and to encourage the investment necessary for the creation of productive jobs for all Americans who want to work . . . .

We have successfully cut inflation by more than half: when I took of-
ice, the consumer price index was rising at 12.2 percent a year. During
1976, the rate of inflation was five percent.

We have created more jobs -- over four million more people have
jobs -- today than the spring of 1975. Throughout this nation today we
have over 88 million people in useful, productive jobs -- more than at
any other time in our history. But, there are still too many Americans
unemployed. This is the greatest regret as I leave office.

We brought about with the Congress, after much delay, the renewal of
general revenue sharing. We expanded community development and Federal manpower programs. We began a significant urban mass-transit program. Federal programs today provide more funds for out states and local
cal governments than ever before -- $70 billion for the current fiscal year.

Through these programs and others that provide aid directly to individuals we have kept faith with our tradition of compassionate help for
those who need it. As we begin our third century we can be proud of the
progress we have made in meeting human needs for all of our citizens. . . .

We have had some successes. And there have been some disappoint-
ments.

Bluntly, I must remind you that we have not made satisfactory progress toward achieving energy independence.

Energy is absolutely vital to the defense of our country, to the strength
of our economy and to the quality of our lives. Two years ago I proposed
to the Congress the first comprehensive national energy program: a specific and coordinated set of measures that would end our vulnerability to
embargo, blockade or arbitrary price increases, and would mobilize U.S.
technology and resources to supply a significant share of the free world's
energy after 1985.

Of the major energy proposals I submitted two years ago, only half belatedly became law. In 1973, we were dependent upon foreign oil imports for 36 percent of our needs. Today we are 40 percent dependent, and we'll pay out $34 billion for foreign oil this year alone. Such vulnerability at present or in the future is intolerable and must be ended. . . .

I set out to reduce the growth in the size and spending of the Federal Government, but no President can accomplish this alone. The Congress side-tracked most of my requests for authority to consolidate overlapping programs and agencies, to return more decision-making and responsibility to State and local governments through block grants instead of rigid categorical programs and to eliminate unnecessary red tape and outrageously complex regulations.

We have made some progress in cutting back the expansion of government and its intrusion into individual lives -- but, believe me, there is much more to be done, and you and I know it. It can only be done by tough and temporarily painful surgery by a Congress as prepared as the President to face up to this very real political problem.

Again, I wish my successor, working with a substantial majority of his own party, the best of success in reforming the costly and cumbersome machinery of the Federal Government.

The task of self-government is never finished. The problems are great; the opportunities are greater.

America's first goal is and always will be peace with honor. America must remain first in keeping peace in the world. We can remain first in peace only if we are never second in defense.

In presenting the State of the Union to the Congress and to the American people, I have a special obligation as commander-in-chief to report on our national defense. Our survival as a free and independent people requires, above all, strong military forces that are well-equipped and highly trained to perform their assigned mission.

I am particularly gratified to report that over the past two and a half years we have been able to reverse the dangerous decline of the previous decade in the real resources this country was devoting to national defense. . .

As I leave office, I can report that our national defense is effectively deterring conflict today. Our armed forces are capable of carrying out the variety of missions assigned to them. Programs are under way which will assure we can deter war in the years ahead.

But I also must warn that it will require a sustained effort over a period of years to maintain these capabilities. We must have the wisdom, the stamina and the courage to prepare today for the perils of tomorrow, and I believe we will.

As I look to the future -- and I assure you I intend to go on doing that for a good many years -- I can say with confidence that the State of the Union is good, but we must go on making it better and better.

This gathering symbolizes the constitutional foundation which makes continued progress possible, synchronizing the skills of three independent branches of Government, reserving fundamental sovereignty to the people of this great land.

It is only as the temporary representative and servants of the people that we meet here -- we bring no hereditary status or gift of infallibility and none follows us trom this place. Like President Washington, like the more fortunate of his successors, I look forward to the status of private citizen with gladness and gratitude. To me, being a citizen of the United States of America is the greates honor and privilege in this world.

From the opportunities which fate and my fellow citizens have given me, as a member of the House, as Vice President and President of the Senate, and as President of all the people, I have come to understand and to place the highest value on the checks and balances which our founders imposed on government through the separation of powers, among coequal legislative, executive and judicial branches.

This often results in difficulty and delay, as I well know, but it also places supreme authority under God, beyond any one person, any one branch, any majority great or small, or any one party. The Constitution is the bedrock of all our freedoms; guard and cherish it; keep honor and order in your own house; and the republic will endure.

It is not easy to end these remarks; in this chamber, along with some of you, I have experienced many, many of the highlights of my life. It was here that I stood 28 years ago with my freshman colleagues as Speaker Sam Rayburn administered the oath -- I see some of you now, Charlie Bennett, Dick Bolling, Carl Perkins, Pete Rodino, Harley Staggers, Tom Steed, Sid Yates and Clem Zablocki, and I remember those who have gone to their rest.

It was here we waged many a lively battle, won some, lost some, but always remaining friends. It was here surrounded by such friends that the distinguished Chief Justice swore me in as Vice President on Dec. 6, 1973. It was here I returned eight months later as your President to ask you not for a honeymoon, but for a good marriage.

I will always treasure those memories and your many, many kindnesses. I thank you for them.

My fellow Americans, I once asked for your prayers, and now I give you mine: May God guide this wonderful country, its people, and those they have chosen to lead them. May our third century be illuminated by liberty and blessed with brotherhood, so that we and all who come after us may be the humble servants of thy peace. Amen.

BIBLIOGRAPHY

Obviously it is far too soon to prepare a critical history of the Ford presidency, or even to prepare a bibliography. The official records of those years are not yet available, and the men who served Gerald Ford are still convalescing from the tensions of the White House. Doubtless they are preparing their thoughts for the books they intend to write. Press attention has centered on Secretary Henry Kissinger, whose promised volume, due in 1979, will shed light and probably controversy on the Nixon-Ford years. Soon many others, in addition to the former presidents themselves, will put their thoughts on paper and provide historians with a mother lode of information which will enable them in turn to complete their own books.

All this is in the future, however, and in 1977 no good history of the Ford presidency or biography of Gerald Ford yet exists. In a sense, it is amazing that a man whose public life extends over twenty-eight years has elicited so little attention from historians. That situation, of course, will soon change. The president has decided that his public papers are to be deposited at the University of Michigan, and has agreed that a museum, dedicated to his career, be someday erected in Grand Rapids. Until these structures rise, there are several other obvious starting points for investigations of the Ford presidency. The Weekly Compilation of Presidential Documents, published each Monday by the Office of the Federal Register, National Archives and Records Service, is essential. Its coverage of Ford begins with Volume 10, Number 32, page 1023 and continues for eight volumes. It gives the student not only the president's words but also a listing of the major events of his day. Many articles about Ford are cited in the Reader's Guide to Periodical Literature and the Social Sciences and Humanities Index; no researcher can do without the Index to the New York Times. Raw material for an examination of Ford's Congressional career exists in the pages of the Congressional Record and is yet to be mined. Like many representatives, Ford inserted into the Record a summary of his important votes -- a convenience to both his constituents and to historians. Continuous coverage of the Ford presidency was the concern of many magazines; their commentary and reportage are perhaps best typefied by John Osborn's "White House Watch" in the New Republic. That column offers a potential biographer many insights into Ford's character and the pressure of the White House.

Listed below are a tentative sampling of the books that have so far appeared dealing with Ford, the merest foretaste of the flood soon certain to appear.

Breslin, Jimmy. How the Good Guys Finally Won. Notes from an Impeachment Summer (New York: Viking Press, 1975). A fun book in which the "good guys" are led by "Tip" O'Neill, Peter Rodino and John Doar. Jerry Ford is treated with fine disdain.

Doyle, Michael V. (ed.). Selected Speeches by Gerald R. Ford (Arlington, Va.: R. W. Beatty, 1973).

Feerick, John D. The Twenty-fifth Amendment. Its Complete History and Earliest Applications (New York: Fordham University Press, 1976).

Ferretti, Fred. The Year the Big Apple Went Bust. (New York: G.P. Putnam's Sons, 1976). An excellent job of reportage which traces New York City's debacle. Ferretti on Ford's treatment of New York -- "utterly disgraceful and totally amoral."

Ford, Gerald R. "What can save the G.O.P.," Fortune, v. 71 (January, 1965).

Ford, Gerald R. "Impeachment - A Mace for the Federal Judiciary," Notre Dame Lawyer, v. 46 (Summer, 1971), 669-677. Discussion of the "political mechanism" of impeachment and its application to "judicial behavior."

Ford, Gerald R. and Stiles, John R. Portrait of the Assassin. (New York: Simon and Schuster, 1965). A review of the 522 witnesses and 25,000 pages of Warren Commission testimony, and a defense of its correct conclusions.

Hersey, John. The President (New York: Alfred A. Knopf, 1975). A Yale man, Hersey likes Ford and reveres the presidency.

Lukas, J. Anthony. Nightmare. The Underside of the Nixon Years (New York: Viking Press, 1975). The best treatment of the "long national nightmare" that Ford lamented upon taking office.

Mollenhoff, Clark R. The Man who Pardoned Nixon (New York: St. Martin's Press, 1976). A too soon, too angry look at "Richard Nixon's revenge."

President Ford: The Man and his record/Congressional Quarterly (Washington: Congressional Quarterly, Inc., 1974).

Reeves, Richard. A Ford, Not a Lincoln (New York: Harcourt Brace Jovanovich, 1975). Ford is ineffective but typically a man of Congress. We must realize that "the President of the United States is a very ordinary man."

Rowan, Roy. The Four Days of Mayaguez (New York: W. W. Norton & Co., 1975). Although hardly definitive, this troubling volume shows how little we understand about decision making. Its analysis questions why Ford should feel any pride in his Mayaguez decision.

Sidey, Hugh. Portrait of a President (New York: Harper & Row, 1975). An analysis of transition, with photos by Fred Ward.

terHorst, Jerald F. Gerald Ford and the Future of the Presidency (New York: The Third Press, 1974). A candid look at Ford by an old pal who resigned in protest when the president's ingrained sense of political loyalty led him to pardon Nixon.

U. S. Congress. Senate. Committee on Rules and Administration. Nomination of Gerald R. Ford of Michigan to be Vice President of the United States, Hearings. (Washington: Government Printing Office, 1973)

Vestal, Bud. Jerry Ford, Up Close. An Investigative Biography (New York: Coward, McCann and Geoghegan, 1974). A curiously "in between" volume on a vice president about to be president. Despite its title, there is no real focus on Ford the man.

Weekly Compilation of Presidential Documents (Washington: 1974-77).

White, Theodore H. Breach of Faith: The Fall of Richard Nixon (New York: Atheneum Publishers, 1975). A despairing look at Nixon by a man who reluctantly had seen his virtues.

Wills, Gary, "He's not so dumb," New York Review of Books, October 16, 1975.

Winter-Berger, Robert N. The Gerald Ford Letters (Secaucus, N.J.: Lyle Stuart, 1974). A lobbyist charges that Ford accepted illegitimate political payoffs.